BBC Book of Golf

*Gary Player pictured against the sea at Turnberry*

# BBC Book of Golf

**Peter Alliss**
**Harry Carpenter**
**Henry Longhurst**
**Mark McCormack**
**Tom Scott**
edited by **Ken Hawkes**

British Broadcasting Corporation

*Peter Oosterhuis*

Published by the
British Broadcasting Corporation
35 Marylebone High Street
London W1M 4AA

ISBN 0 563 12188 2
First published 1975



Set in 'Monophoto' Times New Roman
and printed in England
by John Blackburn Limited,
Old Run Road, Leeds LS10 2AA

# Contents

*Roberto de Vicenzo*

# Foreword

Everyone connected with the transmission of golf on BBC-tv seems to enjoy the game. Most of us play it, some well, some badly. But, whatever our handicap, we hope our enthusiasm for the sport comes across on the 'box' and that it also permeates the pages of this book, which is long overdue. We hope the waiting will have been worthwhile.

My own association with BBC golf coverage is now in its tenth year and I can honestly say I have spent some of the happiest moments of my TV work linking our golf events. As Henry Longhurst always says: We are fortunate that golf takes us to so many beautiful places.

We are also lucky that BBC golf policy concentrates on major events and that we are constantly reporting on the achievements of the greatest players in the sport.

This book, I think, reflects that policy, dealing as it does with the British and US Open Championships, the US Masters and USPGA Championships, the Piccadilly World Match Play Championship and the Double Diamond International Team Championship. These events are the very solid foundations on which BBC-tv golf coverage is based.

Our intention in this volume is, first, to entertain, and, second, to inform in such a way that your appreciation of future golf events on TV may be enhanced. For example, you will find hole-by-hole descriptions of the courses on which the British Open will be decided these next three years.

There are contributions here by our regular team of BBC-tv commentators: Henry Longhurst, Peter Alliss and Mark McCormack, and also from that stalwart of golf on radio, Tom Scott. Here, too, you will find biographies of a hundred of the leading players, a glossary of the terms used by our commentators, and a section of results.

All in all, we hope it's a 'good read', but particularly that it may strengthen a valuable bond between the BBC and the golfing public, many of whom are kind enough to write and tell us they enjoy our efforts.

Long may it continue to be so.

Harry Carpenter

*Tom Weiskopf in action during the 1974 British Open*

# 1 Introduction

# Looking in at golf by Henry Longhurst

The reader will find elsewhere in this book a glossary of golfing terms, but at the risk of duplication I must mention one of them, and the shortest at that, namely *par*. Only the other day I met a man who said he was totally addicted to watching golf on television, thought it was wonderful etc., and then asked me what par was. Par, to put it shortly, is what you might call the 'correct' score for a really good player, not necessarily as good as Jack Nicklaus, but in the very top flight. It is calculated by yardage: holes up to 250 yards, par-3, i.e. one shot and two putts when you get there; up to 475 yards, par-4, two shots and two putts; anything over 475, par-5, three shots and two putts.

Par is now the whole basis of our television score system. It used to be 'level fours', so that a player doing a hole in three would be said to be 'one under fours' for that hole, and 'one over fours' for a hole done in five. You may imagine our difficulties towards the end, when so-and-so was level fours, but with a short hole to come, while somebody else behind him was, say, level fours, but with a long hole to come. To make the necessary calculations and bring in the correct winner, without the aid of today's elaborate scoring systems and 'leader boards', and individual boards carried round with each match towards the end, was no small headache for the commentators of early days. I mention this largely because the issue is now simple for both commentator and viewer to take in. It no longer matters what the individual pars of the holes shown may be. Par is par and that is the end of it, so if a man is, let us say, ten under par when we join him and does a par-3 hole in 3 he remains ten under. If he gets a 2, he goes 11 under. If he takes 4, he goes back to nine under. This system is now standard practice wherever golf is shown on television.

One slight, though very slight, disadvantage is that par by its very nature is static. The 'card of the course', showing the length of the holes and the pars, has to be printed in great numbers and stay the same all the year round. So, while the par may be, say, 72, on the same course in half a gale the 'true' par might be 74 – and in mid-summer, when most television tournaments are played, it may be nearer 69, though I dare say a good many players would not care to be reminded of the fact. At any rate, this explains why one sees players with some prodigious score like 'twenty under par'.

Now to the matter of the golfers' 'style'. So and so, it will be said, has a beautiful style. In my earlier days he would have been known as a 'stylish player'. This is a difficult subject to put into words. Anyone in the world of golf can tell all the best players apart at a distance, not only from their clothes and shape, but from their action in hitting the ball. It might therefore be said that, since all are recognisable in this way, they all have different styles. But if the student of golf will watch carefully – and the television, especially in slow motion, will show him what he cannot see with the naked eye – he will see that they have an astonishing amount in common.

I think it is true, though I say it with some diffidence, that there is now something approaching a 'correct' style, and that if you stood on the first tee of the average golf club on a Sunday morning, you would very rarely see it. Or, to put it another way, if a couple of professionals drove off among all the rest, a comparative novice would instantly detect which they were. You will see on the television that players almost inevitably address the ball (for a full shot, anyway) with the ball just about opposite the left heel, the left arm and the club in a straight line and the left shoulder higher than the right. Having read which, have a look in a full-length mirror and see where yours are!

If you watch the right hip (the left, as you look at it), you will find that on the backswing it does not, as you might think, move back in order to gather momentum: it moves round, as though they were playing in a barrel. Watch this one, too, on a Sunday morning. You will also find that, at the top of the swing, the good player's shoulders have turned so that his back is actually facing the hole and his left shoulder pointing at the ball. Nicklaus is probably the mightiest hitter today and plays well within himself, but sometimes when he really needs the distance he lets one fly. You can always tell when one of these is coming by the fact that he 'winds up' to such an extent that his left shoulder at the top of the swing is actually pointing *behind* the ball.

The great golfing axiom of my youth was, 'Keep your eye on the ball', but it has long since been demonstrated that you can hit the ball very well without looking at it at all. The real axiom is 'keep your head still' and, although elsewhere in this volume you will see that the great Lee Trevino doesn't (he dips his about nine inches as he comes into the ball), this is perhaps the great truth in the golf swing. Furthermore it is one often demonstrable on the television, because we are constantly showing players with their heads against a dark background of woods or bushes. Some of them scarcely move half-an-inch. Here again, have a look at the first tee on a Sunday morning, where you will be able to distinguish another notable difference between 'them' and 'us'. They finish in perfect balance on the left foot: we tend to have hit ourselves backwards on to the right foot, after which some of us, far from being in a poised and elegant position of balance, are pulling the club up and down as though bellringing.

With all this, I have not really begun to define 'style', but I think that if you cast an eye on the points I have mentioned you will detect quite clearly which players have style and which are the more humdrum, however workmanlike, strikers of the ball, just as you immediately can in cricket.

Another point on which the handicap player may care to cast

a special eye will illustrate an elementary truth that escapes many people to their dying day, namely that it is the job of the golfer to hit the ball *forwards*, and the job of the loft on the face of the club to cause it to go *upwards*. Watch a child flipping a stationary table tennis ball back over the net: instinctively he 'lays the face of the club back', as though with the loft of a nine-iron, and then hits forward all along the surface of the table. Watch the good golfer and you will see how, especially with the short irons, the ones calculated to send the ball highest in the air, he is not hitting upwards, but actually hitting downwards, then through the ball. Reverting to cricket again, the ideal golf swing is like hitting a half-volley straight back to the bowler *without giving a catch*. The loft on the club will see the ball safely into the air. Watch this particularly on slow-motion shots.

The business of putting, of which the producer is bound to show a good deal, because it forms such a large proportion of the actual golfing action, is also extremely simple to state, though one may get into a frightful state of nerves over it. It is merely a question of moving a piece of ironmongery to and fro without altering the angle of the face – and here is an interesting thing about television. It shows far, far more clearly than the naked eye, however close you may be standing, when the player alters the angle. Time and again I have found myself saying instinctively, 'Oh, no, no!' before the club has even reached the ball and, touch wood, have always been right.

# 2 The events

*Johnny Miller*

# The British Open Championship by Tom Scott

I was fifteen when I saw my first British Open Championship, or at least part of the great event, not with the permission of my form-master at school, but by my own enterprise, or foolhardiness, call it what you will. Putting it in simple words, I played truant and later paid the penalty with an enormous number of lines, although some practice and a little dexterity made it possible to write two at a time. Despite the loss of leisure, I thought it all well worthwhile.

It was the 1921 Championship at St Andrews in which Jock Hutchison, a local player who had emigrated to the United States, won the title after a play-off with the great amateur, Roger Wethered. Most of my memories of that Championship are happy, but there was a hint of tragedy during the third round, when Wethered accidentally stepped on his ball in the rough and was penalised a stroke. At the end of four rounds the men were level, then Hutchison won the play-off to take the old cup to the United States for the first time. Some held that, had Wethered not suffered the penalty stroke, he would have won – just as, in 1949, others maintained that if the Irishman, Harry Bradshaw, had not hit his ball into a bottle at the long fifth at Royal St George's, Sandwich, he would have beaten Bobby Locke by one stroke, instead of tieing with him and eventually, like Wethered, losing the play-off. Who can tell?

Certainly that first Championship made a great impression on my young mind, but the thought never entered it that one day I would be mixing with the Great Men and counting many of them as personal friends. Some years were to elapse before that happened, but being a keen golfer I went to watch the Open Championship whenever I could, mainly when it was played in Scotland. Bobby Jones's victory at St Andrews in 1927 I remember clearly, although it was not one of his two outstanding successes. They were his momentous win at Royal Lytham in the previous year, after playing a miracle shot from a bunker to the 17th green, which enabled him to beat Al Watrous by two strokes, and his win at Hoylake in 1930, the year of his Grand Slam. But just seeing Jones play was enough. Perhaps it is too much to rate him the greatest golfer who ever lived, but as former Open Champion, Tommy Armour, has said: 'There were none better'.

Of all the Championships I saw between the wars, Henry Cotton's victory at Carnoustie in 1937 stands out most clearly. I regard it as the greatest of Cotton's three wins for two reasons: firstly, the field was the strongest it had ever been and, secondly, Cotton mastered some of the most appalling conditions experienced in the event either before or since.

One more of the 'Between the Wars' era I remember well was in 1939 at St Andrews, when Dick Burton won. Few expected him to do so and many spectators departed thinking the American, Johnny Bulla, would be the victor. But late starter

*Bobby Jones*

Burton finished brilliantly, to hold the title longer than any other man, because of the impending war, whose dark clouds were already rolling across Europe. Even so, I doubt if any of us thought, on that long summer evening, as we gazed respectfully at the Old Course while the little train chugged its way to Leuchars Junction, that so much was to happen before the next Championship would be played, or that some would never see the great event again.

Those of us who did survive the war were delighted that, when the Open started again in 1946, it was once more at St Andrews. True, there was a modest entry, with some of the competitors wearing khaki slacks and pullovers, others the slacks of their demob suits. The great thing was that it took place at all and produced a worthy winner, Samuel Jackson Snead.

But we had to wait another year for the kind of finish dear to the hearts of golf enthusiasts. That was at Hoylake and in those days the winners did not go out last, as they do now. On the final day, a cheerful Irishman, Fred Daly, whistled his way through with seeming unconcern, until he finished in the mid-afternoon with what appeared a winning total of 293.

Some time later an Englishman, Reg Horne, finished one stroke behind, and the only other man who seemed to have a chance was the American amateur, Frank Stranahan. I was with Daly in the clubhouse as the American was finishing his round. 'I can't bear to watch him,' said Daly in his Ulster brogue, 'go and have a look, Tom.'

We knew Stranahan had taken five at the 17th and needed a two at the last hole to tie. I went out to see him play a fine drive to within about 150 yards from the pin. Surely Stranahan had no hope of equalling Daly's score, but we could not be quite sure, so determined was the powerfully-built, dedicated American.

He walked every yard of the 150 yards to the pin, went back to his ball, rolled up his sleeves and hit it as straight as an arrow towards the flag. It landed on the green and ran on and on until it seemed that it must drop into the hole. But it stayed out and I ran back to tell Fred Daly he was champion. The best shot that ever lost a championship? Surely there has been none better.

While we are at Hoylake, let me recall another finish there, 20 years after that between Daly and Stranahan. The central figure was the tall, smiling Argentinian, Roberto de Vicenzo, who had been coming to play in the Championship for a number of years and had been close to winning it several times, only to falter at the last run-in. Now, at the age of 44, he looked like making it at last. At the end of three rounds, he led Gary Player by two strokes and Jack Nicklaus by three. De Vicenzo struck a massive blow, after being in the rough at the 404-yard tenth, when he got his par. The same hole and the next saw Player out of it and only Nicklaus remained to challenge. The American could reduce the leeway by only a single stroke and Roberto became one of the most popular of all winners.

The 1951 Championship had brought a personal milestone, my first radio commentary for the BBC. Some weeks before the event, the first and so far only Open to be played at Royal Portrush in Northern Ireland, I met Henry Longhurst in a favourite West End haunt of ours.

As he was going out of the door, Henry turned and said: 'The BBC are having two commentators out on the course during the Open and I'm going to be the link-man in the clubhouse. Would you care to have a go?'

'Fine,' I replied, 'What will I have to do?'

'Well, when you hear me going over to you, just start speaking and tell us what's happening.'

The time came to climb the scaffolding to my little wooden hut. I was petrified, but all went well until the small boy who was bringing up the scores fell flat on his face at the foot of the ladder. I laid down the microphone, saying 'The small boy who's bringing me my scores has fallen. I'll pop down and get them from him.' With that I jumped smartly down the ladder, leaving the mike to take care of itself. I felt sure my broadcasting career must be nipped in the bud almost before it had begun. But I survived – and have survived other unusual broadcasting experiences as well. But that is another story. At Royal Portrush Max Faulkner was a worthy winner, the last British one we were to see for 18 years.

To see a really great golfer win the title always brings something extra and perhaps the greatest tribute one can pay Ben Hogan for his win at Carnoustie in 1953 is that the knowledgeable Scots had never seen such perfection. Hogan played carefully to one spot on the fairway, to give himself the best line for the shot which followed. They say a great course produces great champions. Carnoustie has produced Tommy Armour, Henry Cotton, Ben Hogan and Gary Player. And they do not come any better than that. Hogan won by four strokes from four men: the amazing Stranahan, who had supplied the drama in that memorable finish at Hoylake; Dai Rees, so desperately wanting the title which has been denied him; Tony Cerda, a charming Argentinian who had been runner-up to Max Faulkner at Royal Portrush; and the young Australian, Peter Thomson. Thomson's first title was to come the following year and he was to be champion five times, more than any other man in the modern era. In fact, only one in any era, Harry Vardon, has won it more often, six times.

Strangely, great sporting events like the Open have a tendency to run in cycles and the nine years between 1952 and 1960 saw the Australians and South Africans dominate it, apart from Hogan's victory in 1953. True, the challenge of the Americans, Hogan apart, was not formidable. But saying that is to do an injustice to Thomson, Locke, Nagle and Player. Thomson won four of his championships in that span, three of them in succession, and he achieved them all with that nonchalant, apparently carefree golf that is his trademark.

No story about the Open can be complete without mention of Bobby Locke, a massive, latterly portly figure, who strode the fairways of the world with a dignity more common among bishops than golfers. His style was not particularly attractive, as he always appeared to be going to hit the ball out to the right. But he never did and, more often than not, he would finish off the job by holing a long putt and lifting his right hand, to touch with the tips of his forefinger and thumb the peak of his white cap. No smile was permitted. The more I think back on the 'characters' the Open Championship has turned up – and there have been a few like the American professional at Royal Birkdale, a year or two back, who in the qualifying test averaged something like six, or was it seven, for the holes played – Bobby Locke gets a place of honour among them.

The little-fancied Kel Nagle took the Centenary Open at St Andrews in 1960, beating Arnold Palmer into second place in a Championship all but ruined by the weather. But Palmer had to wait only one more year to don the mantle of Champion at Royal Birkdale, in another storm-wrecked Championship and a generally unhappy one. The fierce gales and driving rain caused play to be abandoned on the Friday, marquees and refreshments tents were blown down, miserable spectators had few places they could go and generally there was an air of gloom. But Arnold Palmer bore everything with typical fortitude and pressed on to put poor Dai Rees in second place once more. I remember thinking what a cruel stroke of fate it was for Rees to finish with a three which did him no good, when, in 1954, he had ended with a five that cost him the Championship. But that is golf.

The great and popular American did it again the following year at Troon, reversing the first and second placings of 1960. But this time the margin between Palmer and Nagle was the substantial one of six strokes, one of the widest this century.

Bob Charles's Championship at Royal Lytham in 1963 was notable on several counts. He was the first left-hander to take the title and there was a tie, as there had been in the previous Championship at Royal Lytham, when Thomson and Dave Thomas finished level after 72 holes. This time Charles and a chunky American, Phil Rodgers, were in contention. The Royal and Ancient club, smarting under criticism levelled against the 1961 event and, to a lesser extent, Troon in the following year, had wisely decided to make the whole thing more attractive by building big stands, planning a tented village with an exhibition marquee as centrepiece and surrounding it with bars, rest rooms and modern toilets. So the Open moved into a new era.

To some golfers, Tony Lema is just a name. To many, not even that. But I shall always be glad I saw him win his first and last British Open, before tragically losing his life in an aircraft accident. Lema, a tall, softly-spoken man who had come up the hard way, but had the graces of a natural gentleman, was one of the most elegant swingers of a golf club. They had heard about him before he came to St Andrews in 1964 – there are few talented golfers who escape their notice in that golf-minded town – but when I mentioned his name to some of the locals at the bar of the New Club as a possible winner, they laughed. 'He's just arrived and hasn't had a full practice round. No man can treat the Old Course like that and beat it,' they said.

But Lema did just that, to the amazement and delight of all who saw him. In his short trip, Lema had impressed everyone by his bearing and his golf. But even as the crowds hailed him, they were conscious that Jack Nicklaus, in second place, was a coming force.

Not having been enthusiastic about the previous Open at Royal Birkdale, I wondered what the 1965 one would be like, I was happy to find the improvements continued apace, with the tented village bigger than ever and television towers now part and parcel of the scene. But I remember little about this Championship, apart from it being Thomson's fifth win; that Brian Huggett, the tenacious little Welshman who was joint runner-up with Ireland's Christy O'Connor, had four sixes on his last day, and that the name of Tony Jacklin, from Potters Bar, was in the prize list.

And one thing I remember about the 1966 Open at Muirfield was that the Royal and Ancient club had decided to play the Championship over four days, finishing on the Saturday. It proved a great success, so much so that they increased the amount of money paid those in the prize-list, at the head of which was Jack Nicklaus, whom I have always held in the highest regard as golfer and man. He has never caught the imagination of the galleries in the same way as 'Arnie', but I believe by the time Jack has finished with tournament golf, his record will outstrip – and by a wide margin – the exploits of his friend and rival.

Having written of Nicklaus and Palmer, this seems a suitable point to mention the other member of what was once dubbed 'The Big Three', Gary Player. I have known him since he was a boy and had many long talking sessions with him, both because I enjoy his company and because he is what we golf writers call 'good copy'. No matter what the time of day or the situation, whether he has won a tournament or lost it, Gary Player always has plenty to say about the game of golf and his outlook on humanity. At the end of the 1971 Piccadilly Match Play tournament at Wentworth, I incurred the sponsors' displeasure by keeping Gary too long in the BBC radio mobile studio. My defence: 'How do you stop Gary in full spate?'

I am much nearer the close than the beginning of a golf-writing career which has stretched over many years, but though time dims the memory, I am certain the most dramatic Opens I have seen were recent ones: Tony Jacklin's win at Royal Lytham in 1969 and the tragedy of Doug Sanders in 1970 at St Andrews.

By 1969 we were looking on the young man from Scunthorpe as the Big Hope of British golf, the man most likely to wrest the old trophy from the overseas invaders, but I doubt if we thought he would do it quite so soon. That was what made his success, after 18 years of British disappointments, so sweet. I shall never forget that summer evening when he and his partner, Bob Charles, were coming down the 18th fairway, Jacklin with a two-stroke lead. It was a good lead, but what, we asked, if Charles took three and Jacklin five or even a six. Those of us who had watched the Championship on the same course eleven years earlier remembered how one or two players had taken sixes and lost the title.

But Jacklin hit a magnificent teeshot, better than that of Charles, which was to the right. That was one chance of disaster out of the way. Charles's second shot was within holing distance, so Jacklin had to get his on the green. He did, only a little further away than that of his partner, and the crowd knew the moment for which they had waited so patiently was at hand. Much of the tension disappeared and there was laughter as someone, stampeding behind the gladiators, trod on Jacklin's shoe, so that his heel came out of it. With the greatest moment of his young life at hand, Tony bent down, calmly took off the shoe, put it on again and laced it up.

Then, to a crescendo of cheers, the like of which I have never heard in a Championship, he proceeded to get the ball in the hole with two putts. The great scenes on BBC television were doubtless a joy to viewers, but for me the great thing was to be there. Little did we think, however, that within a year Tony Jacklin, OBE, would have joined the ranks of the immortals by being the first British golfer for 50 years to win the US Open Championship and the first British golfer ever to hold both titles at the same time.

Jacklin again made history in 1970 with a first-round score for the first nine holes of the Old Course at St Andrews of 29, almost unbelievable figures. He proceeded back in 3, 3, 4, 4, and was eight under par when a thunderstorm broke over the course and play was abandoned. Next day the holder started where he left off, but the magic of his play had gone, and so, in fact, had his title.

*Agony and ecstasy . . . Tony Jacklin reacts to a missed putt (above) in the 1969 British Open, but he needn't have worried; the broad smile (right) tells its own story of triumph, as he shows the trophy and his winner's medal*

It is not for Jacklin's miracle outward half that this championship will be remembered, however, but for the fact that Doug Sanders, a fine and popular golfer who had never won a major championship, lost the trophy when it was all but in his grasp.

He needed a par four to win at the 18th. He played a good drive, but a somewhat indecisive pitch and run for his second, and the ball ran about eight yards past the hole. His putt was short, woefully short in the circumstances, yet not much more than a yard from the hole. There was a deathly silence as he putted and a gasp of disappointment as the ball slid past the hole. I shall never forget the agony on his face. Somehow I knew that, now he had to have a play-off with Nicklaus, his chance of taking the title he had tried so hard to win for many years had gone.

And so it had. After Sanders had produced a great fight back, Nicklaus, at the same hole which had seen the drama of the previous day, unleashed one of the monumental drives of all time. Standing on the 18th tee, he was one stroke ahead and, with characteristic courage, decided to have a go for the green. In fact, the ball went over the green and Nicklaus was faced with a ticklish shot back. He played it well, then sank the putt for a three. And further salt was rubbed in Sanders's wounds when he, too, got down in three, a three which a day earlier would have given him victory. I still feel sympathy for Sanders, but Nicklaus was a great winner.

The 100th Championship was played at Royal Birkdale in 1971 and, as becoming the occasion, the layout and organisation were bigger and better than ever. In the end we had a sparkling last-round contest, mainly between two of golf's personalities, the irrepressible Lee Trevino, who won his third major championship of the year, and the man who followed him home, Liang-Huan Lu from Taiwan. The courtly little man had captured most of the publicity by doffing his hat at any appreciation of his efforts and he quickly became the darling of the crowds.

Like everyone else, I was ready to accept that Mr Lu, as he came to be called, and his hat had been together for years, until I stumbled on the fact that he hardly ever wore a hat before coming to Birkdale and bought one there only because it was raining on a practice day. I did not have the heart to spoil the image of the charming man who so nearly became champion. In fact, had his ball not struck a woman spectator at the last hole, he might well have done so. As it was, Trevino – the man some said, after he had won his first American Open, would never win another – took the American, the Canadian and the British in one year. And that is a very considerable feat.

*The putt that cost Doug Sanders the 1970 Open Championship. His disappointment is echoed by the crowd on the 18th green at St Andrews*

What is more, he repeated his win in the Open Championship at Muirfield the following year. Again the margin was as

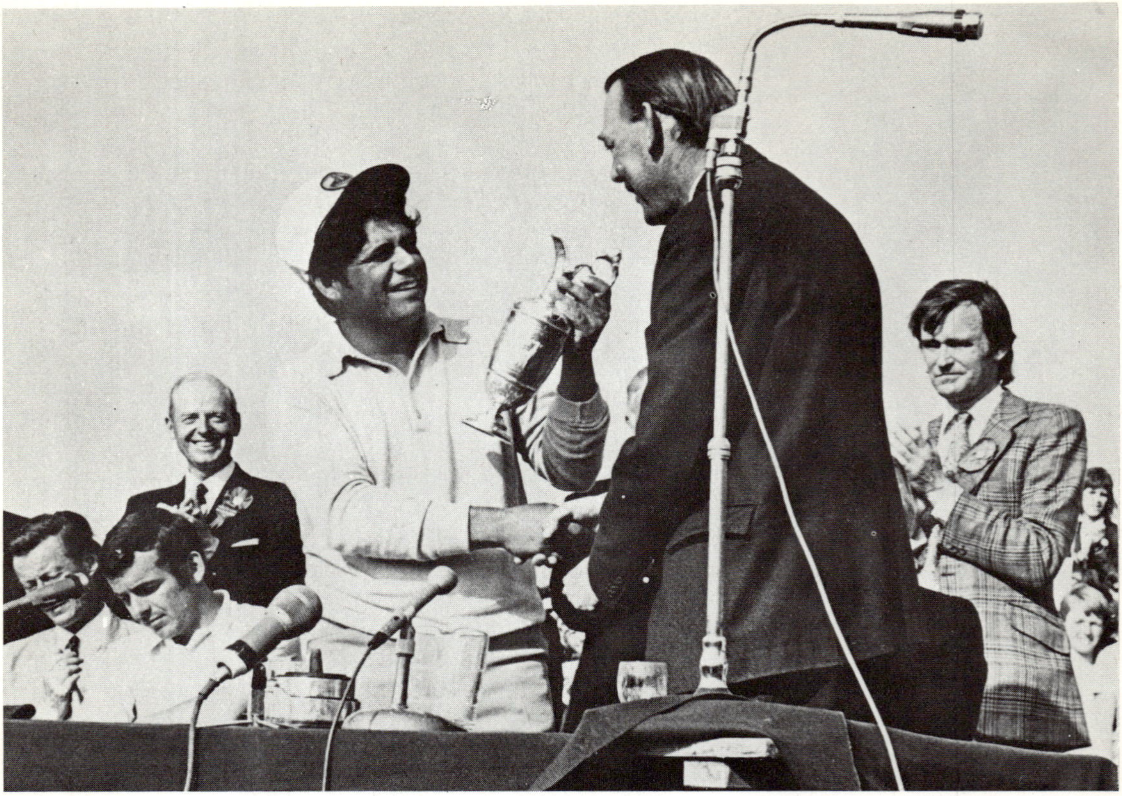

*Lee Trevino collects the British Open Championship for the second successive year, at Muirfield in 1972*

narrow as it could be, but one stroke is as good as a dozen. This time the runner-up was former title-holder, Jack Nicklaus. Britain's Tony Jacklin was in with a chance to win, but a magical sequence of approach shots and putts gave Trevino the title. And, believe it or not, unlucky Doug Sanders had again looked as if the Championship would be his. In the end, he had to be content with fourth place; good player as Sanders still is, I feel the sands are running out for the likeable American.

Illness kept me away from the 1973 Open, which will not be remembered as one of the greatest. The weather was unkind and some felt Troon was not quite up to Championship standard. Not that the course can be faulted, but room at Troon is at a premium for a modern event as big as the Open.

But none could criticise the man who won. For some time Tom Weiskopf had been one of the leading professionals in the United States and the way he won the British title stamped him as a golfer of the highest class. He did what few winners have done – led from start to finish and, in the end, won with an aggregate of 276, the same as Palmer's low record of eleven years earlier. He achieved this in weather which must have been completely alien to him and Weiskopf took his place alongside the best of the Open Champions.

And while a new champion was on his way to being crowned,

an old champion, Gene Sarazen, 71 years of age and playing at Troon 50 years after he had first appeared there, holed out in one. Seeing the ball disappear into the hole on the TV screen was a sentimental moment for me, as it must have been for those who saw it actually happen. Even at second-hand, one of the greatest moments in an event I had been watching for more than half a century lost little of its drama.

Thankfully I was back in action at Royal Lytham the following year and, long before the closing stages, began thinking hard what form my BBC radio interview with the winner could take. 'I have interviewed him so many times,' I said to myself, 'there's nothing left to say to Gary Player.' But experience and luck came to my aid, for after he had stepped off the last green, winner of the Open Championship yet again, he was embraced by his teenage daughter. I took them both into the mobile studio, and, during the interview, asked her what she thought of her father.

'My dad,' she replied, 'is the bravest man in the world. He's the best golfer in the world – and he deserves to win every tournament he plays in.'

Nobody would disagree that Gary Player is a brave man and many would say he is the best golfer in the world. Certainly he made winning the 1974 Open Championship quite a simple affair, starting as he did with two blistering rounds of 69 and 68. At the halfway stage it seemed only a major disaster could

*Gary Player followed his second US Masters win by collecting the British Open for a third time in 1974 – a remarkable achievement after major surgery in the previous year*

relegate him to the also-rans. He did not have a disaster on his third round, but it was a mediocre 75 that enabled Britain's Peter Oosterhuis to get within three strokes of him, with Jack Nicklaus hovering about. Even after Player's bad round, however, not many people present thought deep down in their hearts that anybody could catch him.

I certainly did not and, in the end, the South African went round in 70, while both Oosterhuis and Nicklaus took one stroke more. The spectacle of a young British professional chasing the Great Man was much to the liking of the crowd, and Oosterhuis gave everybody a run for their money, but Player never gave up the initiative. By refusing to get ruffled, by keeping on the attack, he kept the pressure on his challengers.

That is what being a Champion is all about!

# The Piccadilly World Match Play Championship by Peter Alliss

Wentworth Golf Club, in beautiful, wooded country some thirty miles south-west of London, is one of Britain's top golfing centres. My memories of it go back to 1950 and over the years it has brought me much happiness and a few tears. Even now I shudder about putting my second shot into the rhododendrons on the left of the 3rd green, being out of bounds at the 4th, or in one of the lovely gardens bordering the 17th – all that, bear in mind, when I should have been in the middle of the fairway!

Wentworth and I have had a love–hate relationship for years, not because anything is wrong with the course, but because of my own stupidity, lack of finesse or control, call it what you will. As the years go by, however, all the past 7s and 8s fade from memory and one remembers only the 2s and 3s that at the time seemed so infrequent, but have now reached almost overwhelming proportions in the mind.

Many great tournaments and international events have graced the fairways at Wentworth: the Ryder Cup in 1953, and the Canada Cup, now known as the World Cup, in 1956, both historic for different reasons. The Ryder Cup, when Britain had a distinct chance of victory, then, rather like Devon Loch, slipped in sight of the winning post; and the Canada Cup which saw one of the rare appearances in this country of the majestic Ben Hogan; who will ever forget seeing him play round the testing, tough West Course?

These events were grand enough by any standards, but for continuity of spectacle the Piccadilly World Match Play Championship must surely take the cake. This tournament was conceived in 1963 and no one at the preparatory meetings could have visualised the outstanding success it was to become. The concept was unique and original: an event which would bring together the champions of the world. As there was then no world match play event which provided for this, it was agreed on that format, because, of all forms of golf, match play is probably the most exciting.

The thought of seeing those million-dollar golfers fighting man to man, like the barefisted boxing champions of a century or so ago, would, it was hoped, produce an event dramatic and exciting for the players and thrilling for the public. It was a bold step, for Piccadilly, although by most people's standards a vast firm, were among the smallest in their own particular field, and here they were, proposing to start a brand-new venture that would cost a great deal of money.

It was agreed that the ideal number of competitors would be eight and that they should be the leading golfers throughout the world. It was obvious that the American Masters champion, the American Open champion and the British Open champion would qualify automatically. Other choices were more difficult: the British Match Play champion perhaps warranted an automatic invitation, but eyebrows were raised in case somebody won the tournament out of the blue and was not 'One of the World's Best Eight'. Attention was next paid to the American PGA Championship, which had, in a rather checkered career, been both a medal and match play event, and also to the individual trophy of the Canada Cup, as well as to the Open Champions of Australia, New Zealand, South Africa and Canada. From this nucleus the field was to be selected.

It was, of course, easy to leave out some favourites in selecting such an élite gathering, although, on balance, British competitors have shown up fairly well in the event, certainly so far as representation is concerned. In any event, invitations were to be based on competitors' achievements in the preceding year and their general status in international golf.

The field for the first Piccadilly Match Play Championship emerged as the year unfolded. Arnold Palmer, who had been invited on his past record and had shown a positive interest in helping launch the event, dramatically won his fourth American Masters title. The next champion chosen was Ken Venturi, who, after a lean spell, and much ill health, won the American Open. The late Tony Lema won the British Open at St Andrews at his very first attempt, one of the few players ever to achieve that feat; Gary Player was the Australian Open Champion, Bruce Devlin the New Zealand Open Champion, and Jack Nicklaus the individual Canada Cup winner. Neil Coles joined the list through his victory in the British Match Play Championship and Peter Butler, who had played with distinction in the 1964 American Masters, the Carling World Championship, and was beaten finalist in the British Match Play Championship, made up the field.

This exclusive World Match Play group converged on London and the luxury of the Savoy Hotel, where magnificent limousines were laid on for their transport. Everything was done for the benefit of the players, but the sponsors were also mindful of the part spectators would play in this great event, and although one year, due to excessive rainfall, the course took a murderous hammering from the thousands who stampeded along its fairways, spectator comfort at Wentworth has been all-important. Shuttle-service buses helped people find where the action was, ran them back to the clubhouse for a sandwich and beer, ferried them to and from the massive car parks.

The man of the opening tournament was undoubtedly Arnold Palmer. He has often risen to almost unbelievable golfing heights in a tremendous career and he did it again here. Palmer was drawn against Peter Butler in the opening match; it was cut and thrust all the way over 36 holes and, at the end, he won by just one hole. 'He scared the hell out of me' was Palmer's only comment. Gary Player won his first-round match against the ailing Ken Venturi and gave an outstanding display of putting; Tony Lema lost to Neil Coles – a great victory, as Lema was regarded as natural successor to Palmer. The last of the first-round matches brought together the younger generation in Jack Nicklaus and Bruce Devlin, with the latter's cool composure helping him win 3 and 2. Devlin went on to win many of the world's top events, but has never managed to pull off either the British or American Open Championships.

There was an incredible start to the Palmer–Player semi-final. Both are very tough competitors and, although close friends and travelling companions for many years, both love to be top dog. All the friendship was set aside in a brilliant match. Palmer reached the turn in 35, but found himself one down. He did the next 9 holes in 34, and because Player's putting – so devastating in his first-round match against Venturi – was troubling him, went into lunch 4 up. Any hopes of Player recovering were dashed by Palmer's start in the afternoon: he began with an eagle 3, followed with a birdie 2, birdie 4, birdie 4, another birdie 2, and really put the sword in with a birdie 3 at the 6th. Gary could not stand up to that sort of pressure and eventually went down 8 and 6. He has since had his revenge on Palmer, but I know just how much it stung him at the time.

*Wentworth 11 October 1964 . . . Neil Coles (right) congratulates Arnold Palmer on becoming the first Piccadilly World Match Play Champion. Palmer, who beat Coles 2 and 1, took the trophy and £5000 first prize*

In the other semi-final, Neil Coles beat Bruce Devlin in a hard, but not spectacular, match which see-sawed to and fro. Coles, acknowledged expert of the Burma Road, kept his ball in play, hit the greens, putted well and eventually ground Devlin down by sheer persistence and consistency. The final between Arnold Palmer and Neil Coles was an interesting contrast: one a man whose bearing on the golf course could incite thousands of faithful followers to loud cheering and shouting, the other reserved, quiet, dedicated, but one of the toughest men to beat in the game, particularly round this course. But well though Coles played, Palmer was just too strong for him and became the first Piccadilly Match Play Champion. At the prizegiving he was presented with the winner's blazer, in the style of the US Masters. On it was a badge telling the world that here was its Match Play Champion.

Since 1964, among several other winners, Gary Player has almost made it his own event by winning five times. There has been some wonderful golf, much of which I have been privileged to see. The competitors who have graced this tournament – among them Bob Charles, the greatest left-hander the world has ever seen, Lee Trevino, Gene Littler, Gay Brewer, Maurice Bembridge, Tommy Aaron, Ray Floyd, Dave Stockton, Peter Thomson, Billy Casper, Roberto de Vicenzo, Dave Thomas, Tony Jacklin, Jean Garaialde and Brian Huggett – show the quality of the field.

There have been many incidents, among them that in the 1966 Jack Nicklaus v. Gary Player final, when Nicklaus had his

famous confrontation with the referee, Col A. A. Duncan, on whether he could pick up his ball from deep rough for a free drop, because there was an advertising sign some yards ahead and he thought, rightly or wrongly, he might hit it. The sign was certainly there and one *could* say it was in the way, but the ball was reckoned by many who saw it to be pretty well down in the rough – and even the mighty Jack might not have been able to get it out so far. Referee Duncan retired, leaving the match to be finished off by Gerald Micklem, who happened to be standing by.

Then there was the time Gay Brewer and Gary Player had their slight first-round hooha in 1967. On going to the 38th hole in the gathering gloom, they discovered the greenkeeper had cut a new hole for the following day's play, so they were not playing the same course as earlier in the day. Brewer asked for the pin to be replaced in its original position. The referee was that great amateur golfer, Michael Bonallack, who duly brought out his penknife and did a good job of gardening. The hole was replaced, played as it had been intended and halved – but for all his wanting to do everything right, Brewer lost the match at the next hole.

Gary Player has been involved in many incidents over the years at the Piccadilly and no one who was there will forget that at the 37th hole in a 1968 semi-final with Tony Jacklin. After holing his putt, Player went to the crowd to remonstrate with them about alleged remarks someone had made, leaving Jacklin with a three-footer to hole. When the hubbub had died down, Jacklin putted – and missed. Player went on to beat Bob Charles in the final.

The event has generally been blessed with good weather, apart from 1968, when the rains turned most of the course and clubhouse surrounds into a sea of mud, but lessons were learnt from that experience. In fact, lessons have been learnt all round. In the early days, one mighty television tower was placed in the middle of the course between the 8th and 9th fairways; it towered perhaps 150 feet, looking terrifyingly frail, with ordinary ladders strapped vertically to the side, and seemed to sway in the breeze. No wonder Henry Longhurst and Bill Cox asked for danger money.

Like most things, TV facilities have improved with age: now a sophisticated BBC system operates almost wholly from the area of the 1st tee and 18th green. In the control box by the side of the 1st tee is the commentary position, from which information is fed out to the public at home. It houses three or four commentators, plus link-man Harry Carpenter and technicians from score-keepers to map-men, who show you on their beautiful plans where the balls have gone. On the left-hand side of the 18th, down in the trees as you look from the clubhouse, sit the producers, surrounded by their magic

*Jack Nicklaus in deep trouble at the 31st hole during the final of the 1966 Piccadilly*

*Coming events cast their shadow . . . Tom Weiskopf, destined to be British Open Champion the following year, holds the World Match Play trophy he won in 1972*

lanterns, lights flashing, phones ringing, children crying, and though I have seen plenty of TV and how it works over the last few years, it never ceases to amaze me. No matter how many miles of cable are laid, how many bits of metal you stick up in the air, how many sets of headphones are used, or how much shouting is done, somehow or other, when someone in a caravan tucked away in the trees presses a switch, someone standing on scaffolding out in the wilds points one of those monster machines at something or someone, suddenly, bang there in front of you is the most beautiful colour picture! As I am still trying to puzzle out how the telephone works, you can understand how television affects me.

The last three years have brought their own moments of drama in this splendid event. In 1972 we saw the massive arrival of Tom Weiskopf, who was to become British Open champion in the following summer. The 6ft 3in American was a giant among pigmies at Wentworth: no matter how they tried, all fell by the wayside, one after another. In 1973 we had the remarkable Gary Player's fifth victory, after a marathon final against Graham Marsh of Australia. It was a week full of incidents, with Player figuring, as usual, in most of them. Controversial at times, perhaps, but how can you criticise a

*Gary Player at the end of the marathon 1973 Match Play final salutes the crowd (left) and is congratulated by Graham Marsh*

man who wins a major event such as this five times in its first ten years.

There were a whole crop of new names in the field for 1974: US Open champion Hale Irwin, Jerry Heard and Ben Crenshaw from the States; Bob Charles from New Zealand, with the previous year's runner-up, Marsh of Australia, Peter Oosterhuis and Tony Jacklin from Britain and, of course, Gary Player. Jacklin beat Oosterhuis easily and looked set for the final, until Irwin eased him out in the semi-finals. The others all fell by the wayside, so it was an Irwin v. Player final. Will Gary do it yet again, we asked. It certainly looked as if he could, but it was not to be. After a tense, but never exhilarating final, Irwin was home by 2 & 1, or 3 & 1 if you want to be pedantic. Either way, it was a brave win.

So we still have to record a British victory. Neil Coles came the closest in the first year. Since then there has not been a home finalist; only Jacklin in 1968 and 1974, Coles in 1971, and Oosterhuis in 1972 have reached the semi-final stage.

This year, I hope we shall see all the world's greats, Nicklaus, Trevino, Miller and Weiskopf; that way it really will be 'The World Match Play Championship'.

# The Double Diamond International Team Championship by Harry Carpenter

Morning train north from Euston . . . *Telegraph* crossword . . . lunch and half-a-bottle of Beaune . . . Lake District in view on the port side . . . a nap . . . anticipation at Stirling that now we are approaching surely the most splendid inland golfing country in all the world . . . Gleneagles!

How wonderfully old-world it all is. The uniformed chauffeur greeting us at Auchterarder station, the stately drive through the grounds and up to the imposing portals, where the hall-porter makes it his business to remember your name and when you were here last.

For those who have not been lucky enough to experience it, Gleneagles is a vast and gloriously old-fashioned hotel (meant in the most complimentary way) and yet it was opened only in 1924, which is not, to me at least, all that far back, as I was born one year later.

It stands in 700 acres of its own grounds on the threshold of the Scottish Highlands, the Grampians clearly visible on a fine day to the north-west. The land rises and falls in a panorama of glen and loch, pine and fir, distant village and rolling moorland.

I have yet to meet a single person who saw all this on TV and failed to remark how beautiful a place it was. The pictures on television even enhanced, if that is possible, the splendour of the scenery by the simple process of putting a frame round each scene and presenting to the viewer a 'painting' of breathtaking beauty.

Gleneagles is so perfect a setting for golf that one wondered if the paraphernalia of modern 'big' golf might not stick out like a sore thumb, what with tents and caravans, scoreboards and refreshment huts. In the event, it was achieved as discreetly as possible by the Double Diamond people, with one or two exceptions, such as the canvas advertising banners draped untidily on grassy banks where they might catch the camera's eye and, worse, those grossly vulgar, oversized Double Diamond bottles used as tee-markers. Can no one devise something equally eye-catching, but less disfiguring?

On Tuesday and Wednesday, Gleneagles swarmed with golfers: 100 of them, playing in the 36-hole individual event which preceded the team championship. The first day ended in a welter of sentiment and Scotch when John Panton, 57, grand old man of Scottish golf, did a hole-in-one at Wee Bogle (Little Ghost), the 135-yard 16th on the King's Course, to win himself an MGB. Panton's delight was clear and the moment relished all the more for the obvious fact that his ample girth made it about as unsuitable a car as you could choose for him. No matter. He gave it to his daughters.

Next day, Maurice Bembridge had to come back in 32, three under par, if he wanted to beat Bob Charles, who was in at 137. He stood on the 18th tee, with 531 yards to play, needing a four to win. It was all downhill, downwind. Drive, 5-iron, two putts . . . thank you very much. Maurice had £1500 in his pocket and the prospect of another £1000 to go with it if the England team, of which he was a member, could win the team championship.

It was Wednesday evening, I believe, when one of the BBC's beautiful young secretaries ventured on to the pitch-and-putt course outside the hotel, with a golf club in her hands for the first time in her life. The course was deserted. Perfect. No beginner wants to be stared at. Rosemary stood on the first tee, shaped up to the ball, then noticed from the corner of her eye two chaps strolling on to the tee. She stopped. My God, it *was* Tony Jacklin and Bob Charles, out for a relaxed round. Rosemary's companion invited them to come through. Politeness itself, they said: 'No, thank you. Go ahead.' Poor Rosemary. Needless to say, the great men were gallant enough to join in the hunt for her ball in the bushes.

BBC-tv opened up Thursday morning from our studio on stilts at 'Clapham Junction', the busy intersection where the 14th and 17th greens, the 18th tee and the entire BBC complex of vans and cables came together. Henry Longhurst, Peter Alliss and Mark McCormack, happily back with us after a serious operation, moved to battle stations in front of their monitors, while I welcomed viewers to 'Gleneagles, in Perthshire'.

The first telegram was not long in arriving. Did I not know that, with the alterations to county boundaries, Gleneagles was in Tayside? I do now.

The £15,000 Double Diamond International Team Championship is simple enough once you grasp its format, but attempting to explain it in a few, well-chosen words is another matter. As well as I can recall, this is what I said:

'Six teams take part: Scotland (the holders), England (past champions), Ireland, Wales, the Continent of Europe, and the Rest of the World. Over three days, each team will play each other once, and each match will consist of four match-play rounds over 18-holes of the King's Course, man against man. Two points for a win, one for a half. The team with the most points wins.'

Well, perhaps not the best explanation possible, and if anyone can think of a better, taking no more air-time, I should be glad to have it in time for this year. These were the teams:

**Scotland** Brian Barnes (capt.), Bernard Gallacher, David Chillas, Ronnie Shade, Harry Bannerman.

**England** Peter Oosterhuis (capt.), Tony Jacklin, Peter Townsend, Tommy Horton, Maurice Bembridge.

**Ireland** Christy O'Connor Senr (capt.), Christy O'Connor Jnr, John O'Leary, Eddie Polland, Jimmy Kinsella.

**Wales** Brian Huggett (capt.), Craig DeFoy, David Llewellyn, David Vaughan, Andrew Phillips.

**Europe** Donald Swaelens (capt.), Manuel Pinero, Angel Gallardo, Jose Canizares, Jan Dorrestein.

**Rest of the World** Billy Casper (capt.), Doug Sanders, Bob Charles, Dale Hayes, Jack Newton.

England made the perfect start, whitewashing Wales and Europe, winning eight matches for a maximum 16 points. Yet already the tensions of match play were showing. In the morning, Jacklin, playing Llewellyn, was all-square after six holes. He then won three in a row to turn 3 up. A two at the 11th put him 4 up, and a birdie three at the 14th won Jacklin the match, 5 & 4. Sad for Llewellyn, yet it proved to be his only defeat all week.

Oosterhuis's match against Vaughan was even more spectacular. England's captain was 3 down after seven holes . . . and then played the remaining 11 holes in seven under fours to win on the final green!

Christy O'Connor Senior, leading Ireland, decided to leave himself out of the first day's play, and stuck to that decision on Friday and Saturday. In Ireland's match against the Rest of the World, livewire Jimmy Kinsella, who had played in the three previous Double Diamond championships and won 10 of his 12 singles, beating every captain he had faced, lost that record when Billy Casper shattered him 6 & 5, playing inspired golf. Jimmy took it with a smile: 'With a bit of luck, he could have won 9 & 8.'

Doug Sanders played his one game of the tournament this day, losing to O'Connor Jnr. That evening he dropped in at the BBC caravan and told of prolonged surgery on his damaged right arm. This had been his first competition for nearly six months and every shot had been painful. Casper rightly rested him from then on.

That night the BBC got to its ungainly feet on Gleneagles dance-floor over which the strains of Henry Hall's band had once wafted in the late 1920s. The current orchestra, thankfully, was fairly restrained and not too much was done to disturb the haggis and bashed neeps (mashed turnips) which is a speciality of Gleneagles' dinner-table.

**First day's results** England 4 Wales 0

Jacklin bt Llewellyn 5 & 4; Horton bt Huggett 4 & 3; Bembridge bt DeFoy 4 & 3; Oosterhuis bt Vaughan, 1 hole.

Ireland 2 Europe 2

Kinsella bt Swaelens 4 & 3; O'Connor Jnr lost to Dorrestein 2 & 1; Polland lost to Canizares 4 & 3; O'Leary bt Gallardo 2 & 1.

Scotland 2½ Wales 1½

Barnes bt Phillips 7 & 6; Gallacher bt Vaughan 5 & 4; Chillas halved with Huggett; Shade lost to Llewellyn 3 & 2.

Rest of World 3 Ireland 1

Sanders lost to O'Connor Jnr 5 & 4; Casper bt Kinsella 6 & 5; Charles bt O'Leary 6 & 5; Hayes bt Polland 3 & 2.

England 4 Europe 0

Jacklin bt Dorrestein 3 & 2; Horton bt Pinero, 2 holes; Bembridge bt Gallardo 4 & 3; Oosterhuis bt Swaelens 2 & 1.

On Friday, Pakistan would not stop bashing England at the Oval until they had made 600, so the viewers were getting their money's worth, what with Test cricket and our golf. England won again, but Ireland took three points off them, O'Leary beating Horton, and Polland getting a half with Oosterhuis. Poor Polland. He was two up with three to play, but Oosterhuis produced three birdies when they were needed.

Jacklin, who seems to save something for when the TV cameras are on him, sank a 35-yard putt on the 18th to clinch his match with Kinsella.

Llewellyn, having beaten Shade of Scotland on Thursday afternoon, now claimed the scalp of Bob Charles, 3 & 1, the only Welshman to win against the Rest of the World.

Brian Barnes, Scotland's skipper, was 3 up with seven to play against Australia's Jack Newton, who then proceeded to go mad and was only one over threes for the next six holes, to win 2 & 1! Newton had not been asked to play in the Rest of the World's opening match, but won his next four games and finished as the only player with a 100 per cent record, foreshadowing his later success in the Benson & Hedges Match Play Championship.

What a day, too, for 21-year-old David Chillas of Scotland: a half with the mighty Casper, and he had to go round in 69 to do it.

I trust Mr Longhurst will not object if I recount one of his off-mike ad-libs to readers. During one of our leisure spells, when the Test was being shown, a cameraman popped up a shot of an outstandingly well-built young lady on Henry's monitor. I mean, superbly well-upholstered. Henry stared at her for a moment and then muttered: 'Halved in two, I think.'

**Second day's results**

Scotland 2 Ireland 2

Barnes bt Kinsella 4 & 3; Bannerman lost to O'Connor Jnr, one hole; Chillas lost to O'Leary 2 & 1; Gallacher bt Polland, one hole.

Rest of World 3 Wales 1

Newton bt Phillips 3 & 1; Hayes bt Vaughan 7 & 5; Charles lost to Llewellyn 3 & 1; Casper bt DeFoy 3 & 2.

England 2½ Ireland 1½

Jacklin bt Kinsella, two holes; Bembridge bt O'Connor Jnr 5 & 4; Horton lost to O'Leary 3 & 2; Oosterhuis halved with Polland.

Scotland 1½ Rest of World 2½

Shade halved with Hayes; Chillas halved with Casper; Barnes lost to Newton 2 & 1; Gallacher halved with Charles.

Wales 2½ Europe 1½

Huggett halved with Swaelens; Llewellyn bt Gallardo, one hole; Phillips bt Canizares 2 & 1; DeFoy lost to Pinero 4 & 2.

As Saturday dawned, England had 21 points out of a possible 24 and led the Rest of the World by four points. She had to play Scotland, the holders, in the morning, and the Rest of the World in the afternoon. There could have been no better finish.

England struggled against Scotland, coming through 2½–1½, but it could easily have been worse had Jacklin not come up with a birdie at the 18th to halve with Bannerman. That half, and its one point, proved valuable.

The Rest of the World whitewashed Europe, so that at lunchtime, England had 26 points, the Rest of the World 25. That one-point lead meant England had only to halve her match with the Rest of the World to win.

There was a superb opener between Jacklin and Casper, won by the Englishman on the final green. A few minutes later, captain Casper was aboard a helicopter, bound for Glasgow, and a plane to the USA, for an exhibition match the following day! Townsend lost to Newton, but Bembridge completed an entirely satisfactory week by making easy work of Hayes, 5 & 4. England had her two wins. The championship was hers. The team was on to £1000 a man.

If Oosterhuis and Charles, bringing up the rear, understood this, I know not. I do know they treated a huge gallery to a fine match, Oosterhuis retrieving nobly those now characteristic wayward tee shots, and Charles dropping all the putts you expect him to drop. It ended with an honourable half.

**Third day's results**

England 2½ Scotland 1½

Townsend bt Shade 5 & 4; Jacklin halved with Bannerman; Oosterhuis bt Chillas 5 & 3; Bembridge lost to Gallacher, one hole.

*The 1974 Double Diamond Cup presented to Peter Oosterhuis, captain of the winning England team, by Lord Derby, president of the PGA. Other team members are (left to right): Maurice Bembridge, Tony Jacklin, Tommy Horton and Peter Townsend*

Rest of World 4 Europe 0
Newton bt Canizares 4 & 3; Casper bt Pinero 5 & 3; Hayes bt Gallardo, one hole; Charles bt Dorrestein 4 & 3.

England 2½ Rest of World 1½
Jacklin bt Casper, one hole; Townsend lost to Newton 4 & 2; Bembridge bt Hayes 5 & 4; Oosterhuis halved with Charles.

Ireland 2½ Wales 1½
Polland lost to Huggett, one hole; Kinsella bt Phillips 3 & 2; O'Connor Jnr bt DeFoy 3 & 1; O'Leary halved with Llewellyn.

Scotland 2½ Europe 1½
Barnes bt Swaelens 2 & 1; Chillas lost to Pinero 3 & 2; Bannerman halved with Dorrestein; Gallacher bt Canizares, two holes.

And this was the final points table:

| | *P* | *W* | *H* | *L* | *Pts* |
|---|---|---|---|---|---|
| **England** | 20 | 14 | 3 | 3 | 31 |
| **Rest of World** | 20 | 12 | 4 | 4 | 28 |
| **Scotland** | 20 | 7 | 6 | 7 | 20 |
| **Ireland** | 20 | 8 | 2 | 10 | 18 |
| **Wales** | 20 | 5 | 3 | 12 | 13 |
| **Europe** | 20 | 4 | 2 | 14 | 10 |

Four men went through the event unbeaten: Newton, Jacklin, Oosterhuis and Gallacher. Llewellyn's part for Wales was tremendous; he won seven of their 13 points. Here are the individual points:

| **Scotland** | *P* | *W* | *H* | *L* | *Pts* | **Wales** | *P* | *W* | *H* | *L* | *Pts* |
|---|---|---|---|---|---|---|---|---|---|---|---|
| Gallacher | 5 | 4 | 1 | 0 | 9 | Llewellyn | 5 | 3 | 1 | 1 | 7 |
| Barnes | 4 | 3 | 0 | 1 | 6 | Huggett | 4 | 1 | 2 | 1 | 4 |
| Bannerman | 3 | 0 | 2 | 1 | 2 | Phillips | 4 | 1 | 0 | 3 | 2 |
| Chillas | 5 | 0 | 2 | 3 | 2 | Vaughan | 3 | 0 | 0 | 3 | 0 |
| Shade | 3 | 0 | 1 | 2 | 1 | DeFoy | 4 | 0 | 0 | 4 | 0 |
| **England** | | | | | | **Europe** | | | | | |
| Jacklin | 5 | 4 | 1 | 0 | 9 | Pinero | 4 | 2 | 0 | 2 | 4 |
| Bembridge | 5 | 4 | 0 | 1 | 8 | Dorrestein | 4 | 1 | 1 | 2 | 3 |
| Oosterhuis | 5 | 3 | 2 | 0 | 8 | Canizares | 4 | 1 | 0 | 3 | 2 |
| Horton | 3 | 2 | 0 | 1 | 4 | Swaelens | 4 | 0 | 1 | 3 | 1 |
| Townsend | 2 | 1 | 0 | 1 | 2 | Gallardo | 4 | 0 | 0 | 4 | 0 |
| **Ireland** | | | | | | **Rest of World** | | | | | |
| O'Leary | 5 | 3 | 1 | 1 | 7 | Newton | 4 | 4 | 0 | 0 | 8 |
| O'Connor Jnr | 5 | 3 | 0 | 2 | 6 | Casper | 5 | 3 | 1 | 1 | 7 |
| Kinsella | 5 | 2 | 0 | 3 | 4 | Hayes | 5 | 3 | 1 | 1 | 7 |
| Polland | 5 | 0 | 1 | 4 | 1 | Charles | 5 | 2 | 2 | 1 | 6 |
| O'Connor Snr | 0 | 0 | 0 | 0 | 0 | Sanders | 1 | 0 | 0 | 1 | 0 |

So we caught the night train to London . . . we toasted Gleneagles and the Double Diamond Championship in someone's compartment before retiring . . . the general feeling was: 'Can we come back again next year?'. . . now we know . . . we can, but not to Gleneagles . . . this time we look forward to magnificent Turnberry.

# The Ryder Cup by Tom Scott

5 October 1957. Perhaps not a day to be marked for ever as a public holiday, or even for hoisting flags throughout the country, although I like to think that at the Lindrick Club, near Sheffield, the club flag is flown on that day to mark a very special occasion, the winning of the Ryder Cup.

I remember hearing a well-known journalist phoning his piece and saying that, with the British Isles team (I must be careful to refer to our Ryder Cup team as such, lest my Irish friends take offence) being 3–1 down, he was prepared to be buried under a load of compost if the home men gained victory. After the match I think someone actually presented him with a bag of compost to help carry out his promise. All good fun that added to the gaiety of a great occasion.

To go on with the story, Saturday dawned pleasant, if somewhat breezy, with a huge crowd turning up and hoping against hope a near miracle would take place. They had not long to wait, for waves of cheers soon came rolling from the first green. The first at Lindrick is a par four and on the previous day the Americans had managed to get down in a succession of birdies. Now the boot was on the other foot and man after man of our side got his three and, in some cases, won the hole.

We could hardly have had a better man at the top than Scotland's Eric Brown, who later was to captain the team with distinction. His opponent was the fire-eating American, Tommy Bolt, for whom he did not care particularly and I doubt if there has ever been such an aggressive display of golf. Brown unleased the full fury of his attack against Bolt. The Scot, confident no American could beat him in a Ryder Cup single – and none ever managed to do it – was four up and set for the kill, although to his credit Bolt hung on manfully, eventually to accept defeat grudgingly on the 15th green.

Having given his team a good start, Brown stayed out on the course and joined Max Faulkner to cheer on the others. They responded magnificently and, at the end of the day, Peter Mills, Ken Bousfield, Dai Rees, Bernard Hunt and Christy O'Connor had all won and the cup had come home after 24 years.

To me, the Lindrick Ryder Cup match will always be something extra special, although there were many before it and there have been a good many since.

The cup was donated by Mr Samuel Ryder, a seed merchant in St Albans, a shy little man with a heavy moustache, who always wore a trilby hat. He was no extrovert, but loved golf, especially professional golf. I think, too, he loved his fellow men and thought what a fine thing it would be if the golfers of Great Britain (as the team was then called) and the United States got together in combat in alternate years.

He loved professional golf well enough, incidentally, to engage as his private professional the great Abe Mitchell.

The first Ryder Cup match was at Worcester, Massachusetts, in 1927. But what might be called its forerunner was played at Wentworth on 4 and 5 June 1926 and the result, for those who have not heard of it, will be a complete surprise. Great Britain won by 13 matches to 1, rather better than we did at Wentworth in 1953, when we lost when we might have won. And make no mistake, in 1926 the Americans had a strong side, including such giants of the game as Tommy Armour (who had five years earlier played for Britain as an amateur against the United States), Jim Barnes and Walter Hagen, all of whom had been, or were to be, American and British Open champions. In addition there were Cyril Walker and Fred McLeod, both United States Open champions.

Mitchell and George Gadd, later to be professional at Roehampton, had big wins, but it was left to Arthur Havers, who had won the Open Championship in 1923, to register the biggest win – 10 and 9 against Fred McLeod. I need hardly say all the matches, foursomes and singles, were 36-hole affairs.

I only regret that my old friend, the late Archie Compston, was the man whose defeat at the hands of a character known as 'Wild Bill' Melhorn, prevented a 'whitewash'. Archie never liked to be reminded of this and his language whenever the subject was brought up was such that few ladies in that unpermissive age would have understood it.

The first official match, with the trophy at stake, ended in victory for the Americans by 9 matches to 2 with one halved. It was a major turnabout from Wentworth but the great international encounter was now launched.

From the inception of the matches until 1961 the format was the same. Play was over two days. On the first day four foursomes were played over 36 holes and on the second day eight singles were played, also over 36 holes. Ten men were chosen for each team and the respective captains were at liberty to use all ten if they cared to do so, or to play the same eight men in the foursomes and in the singles.

In 1961 for the match at Royal Lytham and St Annes the foursomes and the singles were reduced to 18-hole games, two sets of foursomes being played the first day and two sets of singles the second day.

This arrangement lasted for only one year, and when the next match was played at Atlanta, Georgia, in 1963 matches were over three days, two sets of 18-hole foursomes being played the first day, two sets of 18-hole fourball matches the second day and two sets of 18-hole singles the third day. This format has been used ever since with each country being allowed to choose up to twelve players.

Since the event began the captains are allowed to be either playing or non-playing. But now the tendency is to have non-playing captains.

*Something to celebrate . . . Peter Alliss (left) and team captain Dai Rees shake hands after Britain's last Ryder Cup win at Lindrick in 1957. Between them is Max Faulkner, also a member of the successful team*

*British captain George Duncan (right) receives the Ryder Cup from its donor, Mr Samuel Ryder, at Moortown, Leeds, in 1929 – the first time the match was held in this country*

We did rather well in the early matches and, by 6 matches to 4 (2 halved), won the second one at Moortown, Leeds. The old British stalwarts were again on duty, but second last in the singles list was a name which was to become a household word in British golf, the man who, perhaps more than anyone else, would take professional golfers out of the cloth cap era and give them real standing in the game, T. H. Cotton. Cotton justified the confidence invested in him by winning his match.

The next match, in 1931, was lost, but two years later in Britain we got home by a single point in an exciting encounter. That was at Southport and Ainsdale, where the club officials, anticipating big crowds, had enlisted members and supporters, each carrying a long staff with a pennant at the top, to act as stewards. They became known as the Southport Lancers and did a splendid job.

Certainly there were big crowds to control, but how many came to watch the golf and how many to see the Prince of Wales presenting the trophy is a moot point. But present the trophy the Prince did – and to the captain of the home team, the great John Henry Taylor. As he accepted the trophy, I was near enough to see tears glistening in his eyes. There was nothing weak or wrong in that. He had led his team to a great victory.

But if J.H. took the trophy, the hero of the whole affair was Syd Easterbrook of Britain. He was opposed to Densmure Shute, who was to go on to win the Open Championship at St Andrews in the same year. With the whole encounter all square and the match between Shute and Easterbrook all square with one to go Shute was faced with a five-footer, putted and missed. Now Easterbrook had a putt of four feet or a little more to win the hole and clinch the match. It has often been said that Britain produces the man to match the occasion. Certainly it was true this time, for Easterbrook holed the putt.

Although we are proud of attendances at contemporary Ryder Cups, there was one day in that memorable match at Southport and Ainsdale when 18,000 paid for admission. That was remarkable considering there were precious few other amenities. Indeed, it was not until 1965 that the British Professional Golfers' Association got down to staging the great event in a manner worthy of it.

The man responsible for the revolution was not a PGA man at all, but a shrewd Scot, Binnie Clark, an executive for a tobacco firm, which had staged the first tournament at Dalmahoy near Edinburgh in 1963. Binnie Clark, horrified at what passed for spectator amenities, drew up plans for a tented village and these were to become blueprints for later Open Championships and Ryder Cup matches. The 1965 match had a private sponsor in a Royal Birkdale member, Brian Park, who enthusiastically took up what Clark started. The innovations were a huge success, but unhappily the thought and care that had gone into the organisation was not reflected in the performance of the British team.

Harry Weetman and the great American professional, Byron Nelson, were the captains. The result was a win for the Americans by 19½ matches to 12½.

We did well enough the first day, finishing all square, but thereafter the Americans were in front in every series – and that is about all there is to say. I have just been rereading an excellent book by Geoffrey Cousins and Henry Longhurst but not even those experienced writers could make that match exciting. The fact is, we did not have a very good side, while the Americans, including Arnold Palmer, Julius Boros, Tony Lema, Dave Marr, Billy Casper, Ken Venturi and Gene Littler, were very strong.

Byron Nelson told me he thought the match was much closer than the result suggested (remember the 3-day format of 18-hole matches was in operation) but then he always has been a nice man! It has to be said, however, that the golf was of a very high standard and the home men lost to some superb figures. So we went home, saying, 'Well, never mind, they won't beat us when they come to Britain next time.' And they didn't.

Although we lost the 1967 match at Houston, Texas, by the

substantial margin of 12 matches to 2 with two halved, our hopes were high at Royal Birkdale in 1969. We had a strong, young side – half of them under 25 – and, more important, were fortified with the knowledge that the British Open champion, Tony Jacklin, was in the team. Two tough men, Eric Brown and Sam Snead, were the respective captains and both teams had equally tough competitors in their ranks. It was all set for a close, stirring encounter. And so it proved.

The first day was bright and clear, large crowds rolling up, and all went well for the home side, who had a one-point lead at the end of the two series of foursomes. That promised fireworks for the second day – and that is what we got, after the British Isles team had increased their lead by a single point in the morning.

The match which caught the imagination of the public was the second of the afternoon fourballers, in which Brian Huggett was paired with young Bernard Gallacher, a fighting Scot cast in the same mould as his captain, Eric Brown. Right from the start there appeared to be needle in it, Ken Still, a fast-talking, explosive man, displeasing the crowd by his remarks.

On the seventh green, the fire which had been smouldering from the start of the round burst into flame. Dave Hill, the other American, putted out of turn and Huggett at once pointed it out to the referee, David Melville, the professional of the La Moye Club in Jersey. Melville, a quiet, unobtrusive man, was the last person to want to be involved in a row of any sort. But before he could take any action, Still inaugurated what can only be described as a 'heated exchange of words', which ended

*Trouble on the green . . . American Ken Still (second from right) argues with Britain's Brian Huggett at Royal Birkdale in 1969*

with one of the Americans shouting, 'If you want the hole that badly you can have it'. With that, they picked up the ball and stalked off the green, with the hole automatically going to the two Celts, making the score one hole up for the Americans, instead of two up.

At the next, Gallacher conceded Still's putt, mainly, I suspect, to prevent the American from giving his partner the correct line. As Gallacher picked up the ball, Still claimed the hole, saying the Scot had interfered with his ball. The atmosphere was distinctly cool and remained so for the rest of the match which, incidentally, Still and Hill won.

The whole scene was out of keeping with the occasion and afterwards it was forgotten, the adversaries putting it down to pressures on the players. Fortunately such incidents have been few and far between in Ryder Cup matches.

After two days' play, the teams were level, with six games each and four halved and all to play for on the last day, which produced as good golf as any I have seen and an extraordinary climax involving America's greatest golfer, Jack Nicklaus, and Britain's greatest golfer, Tony Jacklin.

The morning matches had gone our way and at lunch we held a lead of two points, the result of a great fight back by the home men, who won the last four singles, Jacklin trouncing Nicklaus 4 and 3 in a match where the American was hardly at his best.

The draw brought the same two into opposition in the afternoon. The big crowd, expecting a stirring struggle, were not disappointed. With three holes to go the match was level with, as it turned out, everything depending on the game. Before the climax came, however, there was a moment of drama, in the match in front, when Brian Huggett, thinking he had to hole a good putt for the whole match, did so, only to discover it was still in the balance.

Just then there was a great shout, as Jacklin got down at the 17th to level with Nicklaus, who had won the 16th.

Both men hit good drives at the 18th and both reached the green with their seconds. Jacklin was 20 feet away, Nicklaus 15. Jacklin to putt first and, in absolute quietness, he sent the ball on its way, to see it finish two feet short. Would Nicklaus hole his and cheat us of the victory all present thought we deserved? He failed, by going four feet past, got down his next and conceded Jacklin's putt, so the whole thing was a tie.

Jacklin told me afterwards: 'Jack and I are great friends and I was pleased, really pleased when he holed the last putt. He had the whole country on his back and he holed out like the man he is, then walked over to me and said "I would never make you hole that one".'

The captain, Eric Brown, said: 'I'm really proud of my boys. I believe we have a wonderful chance of winning the next one.'

*The British Ryder Cup team, who tied the 1969 match, get a big hand after going so near to victory*

Well we didn't win the next match, played at St Louis, but we put up our best ever show in the United States, losing by $18\frac{1}{2}$ points to $13\frac{1}{2}$.

For 1973 the venue was the famous Muirfield, the old club thus having the honour of staging the first Ryder Cup match in Scotland. The Americans produced a strong team, but the home side, chosen from the top men in the Order of Merit, seemed lacking in depth, because one or two hardy match players had not been able to collect enough points during the season.

But all doubts about the quality of our team vanished after the first day, when the British and Irish players established a lead of $5\frac{1}{2}$–$2\frac{1}{2}$ over the Americans. This was a tremendous feat and many home supporters were jubilant, apparently thinking the Cup was as good as ours. Those who, like myself, had seen many Ryder Cup matches were more sober in our assessment – and certain the visitors would stage a fight-back, which was exactly what they did. At the end of the second day they had made up the leeway. The scores were level with everything to play for on the last day.

It was soon clear that some of the home players were exhausted and the captain, Bernard Hunt, realising he had no great strength in depth, was forced to field men who would have been better rested. But he had no option. He had been forced to adopt the same plan on the previous day and now some of his troops were unable to meet the enemy straight on. In the end it was the same old story – a win for the United States by 13 matches to 9.

# The American Scene by Mark McCormack

Golfers, like most humans, are driven by different urges. For the very best of players, however, the chance of immortality overshadows the prize of the moment – the chance to have their names remembered as the Vardons and Taylors, the Joneses and Hagens, the Hogans and Sneads, the Palmers and Nicklauses are remembered. The one sure way to win that immortality is to win a major tournament.

In the early years of golf, before World War I, the British Open was the ultimate goal. In the 1920s the emphasis shifted to the United States Open, and today it is still the most important of them all. Of the world's four major championships three are American: the Open, the PGA and the Masters.

The Open is the oldest tournament in existence in the United States. It began in 1895 and is run by the United States Golf Association. The PGA Championship began in 1916, and behind it is the Professional Golfers Association of America. The Masters was originated in part by Bobby Jones; it has been played since its beginning in 1934 at the same location, the Augusta National Golf Club, one of the finest courses in the country, and it, too, has had a continuing organisation behind it, directed by Clifford Roberts.

## The US Open

Today the US Open, which is moved around the country from year to year, can be entered by professionals and low handicap amateurs, but the final entry is limited to 150, who qualify either by automatic 'exemption' through their records or, the lesser players, by regional and sectional qualifying competitions.

It is a four-day, four-round, 72-hole tournament with a 'cut' to the lowest-scoring players after two rounds: in other words, the same pattern as the British Open. It wasn't always like this.

The Open was born as an afterthought to the principal order of the day – the US Amateur Championship. The first Open was played in 1895 as a sideshow to the Amateur. The USGA had been formed only the previous December so that an amateur championship could be played under circumstances that were acceptable to old Charles Blair Macdonald, who had lost two previous 'national amateur championships'. His first complaint was that a championship could not rightly be settled by stroke-play, the format of the first tournament. Another 'amateur championship' was held later in the year, this time match play, and once more Macdonald lost. Now he complained that one club – in this case, St Andrews in Yonkers, New York – could not properly conduct a national tournament. There must be a national organisation to conduct championships.

*This section is based on chapters in Mark McCormack's book,* The Wonderful World of Professional Golf *(Atheneum, New York).*

J. H. Taylor

Thus was the USGA born, and the following October, 32 players met at the Newport Golf Club in Rhode Island to settle the championship of the land. On 3 October Macdonald finally won the Amateur and peace came over the country.

The Newport Golf Club had a nine-hole course, and the next day professionals were invited to play for the 'Open' championship. Ten pros and one amateur played four times around the nine holes, and when it was over Horace Rawlins had shot 173 for 36 holes to win by two strokes over Willie Dunn. Rawlins was a twenty-one-year-old Englishman who was serving as an assistant at Newport, and he did not shoot any nine holes under 41. It should be remembered, though, that this was the day of the gutta-percha ball, the ground was awfully rough compared with golf courses as we know them today, and the competition was not all that keen.

The game had been introduced into the States only seven years before. The best players of that time were of British origin and British-born players continued to dominate the Open through those early years. Willie Anderson won four times, three years in succession from 1903 through 1905; Harry Vardon came over to play a series of exhibitions in 1900, stopped off in Chicago with J. H. Taylor, a member of the Triumvirate, and the two finished first and second. Laurie Auchterlonie won, and so did Fred Herd and Joe Lloyd, Willie and Alex Smith, of that great family of Carnoustie golfers, and Alex Ross and Fred McLeod.

The man who broke the run, in 1911, was Johnny McDermott, a native Philadelphian who had learned the game in the caddy yards. He was a cocky 19-year-old who thought he could beat everybody and the truth was he just about could. This was a really significant day for American professionals; it was the end of domination by British golfers, a fact that was not really appreciated until two years later at The Country Club in Brookline, Massachusetts.

When McDermott won in 1911 and again at the Country Club of Buffalo in 1912, he beat those British players who had come over to America to live; no one had yet beaten those strong British players who remained at home and who played among themselves. They were, without question, the finest golfers of their era, and at that time the only golf title really worth holding was the British Open. Occasionally they would come over to play exhibitions, as Vardon and Taylor had in 1900, but they were never here during the Open. Then in 1913 Vardon and Ted Ray came to play another exhibition series, and, incidentally, a few tournaments, among them the Open. This was quite an occasion, for the American players felt they were being challenged.

Among the entrants was Francis Ouimet, a twenty-year-old Boston amateur. He nearly withdrew. It is difficult to believe

Harry Vardon

that he had any thoughts of winning, for Vardon and Ray were here, and so were McDermott, Mac Smith and Alex Smith, McNamara, Sargent and a young Rochester professional: it was Walter Hagen's introduction to national competition.

By 1913 the Open had grown so that 36-hole qualifying rounds were needed to cut the field to workable size. Then the field turned to the real competition, two days of 36 holes each over a difficult par 71 layout with the ground softened by rain. Incredibly Ouimet tied with Vardon and Ray, met them in an 18-hole play-off and proceeded to play the extra round in 72 to beat Vardon by five strokes and Ray by six. Never again would the British come to the United States with such confidence; nor would they have reason to be confident for 50 years.

The news of Ouimet's victory sped across the country, and was read by some budding young golfers. It was read in Atlanta by eleven-year-old Bobby Jones. Before Jones's time, though, Walter Hagen made his impact. Hagen had finished fourth in his first attempt at Brookline the year before, just behind Ouimet, Vardon and Ray, and now in 1914 he won. The career of the most flamboyant personality in golf history had been launched. By 1919, when he won the title again, Hagen was acknowledged to be the finest professional golfer in the land.

Prize money in the Open had been increasing steadily ever since it began. While Horace Rawlins had been awarded $150 and a $50 gold medal for winning the first Open, Hagen won $500.

Soon, in England, an event took place that was to change the complexion of golf throughout the world. Hagen had won the British Open a few weeks earlier at Sandwich, and when he did the United States Open became the most important championship in the world. Now it would become a struggle for the British to win their own championship.

Bobby Jones was about to take over. Before *he* could win the British Open, he finally broke through in the United States. Ever since he was fourteen, in 1916, Jones was expected to do great things. He came to Inwood, on Long Island, New York, in 1923 still without a national title after seven years of trying, finally in control of a burning temper that caused him more trouble than any of his opponents.

The championship again hinged on a play-off, Jones versus Bob Cruickshank, and as they stood on the 18th tee they were once more even. Cruickshank was up first and hooked his drive low and left into the rough. Jones hit his drive along the right side, and it came to rest on bare dirt at the edge of the rough. Cruickshank could only play a safety shot short of the lagoon, thus giving Jones an opening, if he could take advantage of it. Hardly hesitating, Jones whipped a mid-iron from his bag and played the shot that changed the course of golf in America, a low, boring shot that screamed toward the green and rolled 6

*Walter Hagen pictured during the 1926 British Open at Royal Lytham and St Annes*

*Ben Hogan*

feet from the hole. Jones had won the Open, and from that moment until his retirement after the 1930 season, Jones dominated world golf.

In 1925 he lost the Open in a play-off, and made an absolute shambles of the competition in the next five championships, winning three of them and losing a play-off in another. He won the British Open for the first time in 1926, then added the US Open later, the first time anyone had ever done it.

The 1930 event was Jones's last Open; later in the year he won the Amateur and completed the Grand Slam, the world's four major championships in one year, a different version from the one we know today but one that may never be done again. With that Jones retired from serious competition and golf went into a period of decline.

With the onset of America's entry into World War II, that era had come to an end. The country was well on its way out of the Depression, and some really great players were beginning to develop – Snead, Nelson, Horton Smith, Jimmy Demaret, Lloyd Mangrum and the Texan Ben Hogan, who became recognised as the best player on the tour and finally broke through to win the Open in 1948.

In 1947 Open prize money had gone into five figures for the first time. The USGA put up $10,000, and the winner, Lew Worsham, received $2000, a heady amount for those times. Something of greater significance happened at the St Louis Country Club that June. A television camera was set up in the back of a truck behind the 18th green – just one camera feeding a local station, which in turn fed 600 television sets in St Louis, a lot of them in saloons, but that one camera was the beginning of modern professional golf. That one camera would transform the $10,000 prize money into the $200,000 purses that are so common in the 1970s.

But in 1948, as I have said, Hogan finally had broken through, and who knew what he might accomplish. One evening in 1949 he and his wife Valerie packed their Cadillac and began to drive home. The night was black, and ghostly ground fog covered West Texas. As they neared the small town of Van Horn, Hogan was creeping along, barely able to see the road ahead. Suddenly from out of the mist two lights bore down on the Hogan car; they belonged to a Greyhound bus and there was no way to avoid a crash. The car was a wreck and Hogan was little more than that. He suffered a double fracture of the pelvis, a broken rib, a broken collarbone and two other injuries that would haunt him the remainder of his competitive career – a broken left ankle and some damage to his left knee. He was alive, all right, but some serious questions were raised that he would ever walk again.

A month after the accident Hogan's condition became quite serious. Blood clots began to form and doctors performed a two-hour abdominal operation tying off the principal blood vessels in his legs. His life was saved once more, but now serious competitive golf was out of the question. Golf once more was without that one dominating personality or impassioned rivalry that so attracts the attention of the sports fan.

Yet by the time the 1949 Open was played, Hogan was out of bed after 58 days on his back, and playing golf – not tournament golf, but a few holes now and then. His strength was coming back and he was regaining most of the 20 pounds he had lost when he was bedridden. He played his first tournament the following January, and in perhaps the most amazing comeback in sports, tied Sam Snead for the Los Angeles Open. Snead won in a play-off, but the whole world knew that Hogan was back.

The 1950 Open was played at the Merion Golf Club on Philadelphia's Main Line. With Pebble Beach, it ranks as one of the two finest golf courses in the country. Hogan played – and won! Before he went on to the course each day he had to wrap his aching legs in yards of elastic tape and at night he had to soak in a hot tub to ease the pain.

The Age of Hogan had arrived, and for the next six years it was Hogan against the field. He was favoured to win every tournament he entered, just as Jones had been 20 to 30 years before, just as Palmer would be in the 60s, and Nicklaus in the 70s. All told Hogan won the Open four times.

By 1959 it was becoming quite evident that golf was about to enter another age. Golf in the post-war era can be divided into three periods: the Age of Hogan, the Age of Palmer and the Age of Nicklaus. For one glorious moment in 1960, all three came together in the Open at the Cherry Hills Country Club in Denver. It was the last dying gasp of Hogan, the first glimmer of the marvellous potential of Nicklaus and the brightest moment in the era of Palmer.

As the final round began Nicklaus, 20, and Hogan were equal fifth, three shots behind the leader Mike Souchak, but Palmer was seven strokes behind, and even his most dedicated followers were not giving him a chance to make up those strokes. Jack and Ben both got into winning positions but it was Palmer who won! He had come from seven strokes off the lead and he had passed 14 other players in one stirring round. A lot of the Palmer legend was born that day and it seemed as if he could go on for ever.

In a sense he has. But in the US Open? Twice in the next three years he tied for the championship and lost in play-offs. Then in 1966 he had the championship in hand, only to lose seven strokes in eight holes to Billy Casper and again lose the play-off. In 1972 he closed in only to finish third.

By 1965 something had happened to the Open. Prize money

was up to $124,000 in the Championship proper and another $7800 in sectional qualifying, which was good, but instead of that double round on Saturday the tournament had been extended to four days, 18 holes a day. The day that seemed to be the single most exciting day in American sport was gone; now they played the Open just like they played the Tucson or Pensacola or Quad Cities Open. True, some, perhaps most, players like it this way, but when the USGA changed the format of the Open, the tournament lost something. It was no longer unique. However the Open had been shown on TV only on Saturday; now it could be on both Saturday and Sunday.

By then we had arrived in the Age of Nicklaus. Of course there have been other champions in between – notably perhaps the ebullient Lee Trevino (twice), Billy Casper, Johnny Miller, the young 1973 winner, and two overseas players, Gary Player and Britain's Tony Jacklin – but Nicklaus has invariably been the man to beat. In 1962 he beat Palmer in a play-off, in 1967 he had a final round of 65 to beat Hogan's record of 276, in 1971 he lost the play-off to Trevino and in 1972 he won again.

With that victory, Nicklaus had matched the record of Bobby Jones, with 13 victories in major competition. It was the third Open for Nicklaus. Only Jones, Hogan and old Willie Anderson had won four, and when the big red sun dipped into the Pacific that night, Jack was only thirty-two, and there was hardly any doubt that he would win more Opens.

Golf, though, is an unpredictable game. What about Sam Snead? Didn't everyone think he would win more than one Open, and didn't he fail to win any? And what of Hogan? Did he not have his finest year in 1953, winning the Open, the British Open and the Masters, and did he not fail to win ever again? And then what of Palmer? Who would have considered that when he played so well at Augusta in 1964, hitting shots as he had never hit them, he had won his last major tournament? Who would have thought?

**The US Masters**

Everyone has his own first sign of spring – onion grass in the garden, a pretty girl in a cotton dress, exhibition baseball games in Florida – but for some the first sign comes early, sometimes just after the first of the year. It is usually in the form of a bulletin, decorated with an outline of the United States, with a flag protruding from the south-east part of it, just about where Georgia is. Written over all this is 'Augusta National Golf Club'. The first bulletin is a reminder that the Masters is coming, and if the Masters is coming, then surely so is spring.

If you have been to Augusta in April, if you have sat beneath the huge magnolia trees on the veranda of the clubhouse or strolled through the tall pine forests and breathed the sweet scents of dogwood and azaleas, you know that there is no golf tournament in the world as special as the Masters.

You cannot make a move around the clubhouse area without encountering some sort of tradition. But the most famous Masters tradition of all, certainly the most cherished and desired, is the awarding of the green jacket to the winner. On Sunday, minutes after the final putt, officials of the club, headed by Clifford Roberts, assemble on the practice putting green, along with the new champion, the old champion, the low amateur and that player or players who have contributed to the excitement, usually someone who has finished second. In that setting, with the spring light fading, the old champion helps the new one slip into his jacket, and no matter how many golf tournaments you have seen or covered, it is a moment that stirs the emotions.

It could be argued that the Masters began in 1930, the moment Bobby Jones sank his final putt at the 11th hole at Merion to beat Gene Homans 9 and 7, win the US Amateur for the fifth time, and wrap up his Grand Slam. With the completion of the Slam Jones retired from competitive golf, although he remained very much involved in the game. He had let it be known that he was interested in the building of a championship course somewhere in his native southland, a course that would conform to his own high standards.

Enter Clifford Roberts, a tall, thin Wall Street investment banker who had long been going to Augusta as a winter vacationer. Roberts knew of Jones's desire to build a course, and so late in 1930 he paid him a visit in Atlanta with the idea of organising and building a club near Augusta. Both Roberts and Jones had a number of friends among the permanent and winter guests who could be counted on to form a nucleus of club members. The rest of the members would come from around the country – a truly national club, as the name Augusta National implies; a retreat where, as Jones once wrote, 'men of means might play with kindred spirits'.

One chilly December morning in 1930, Clifford Roberts and Alfred Bourne, a member of the Singer Sewing Machine family, took Jones to a 365-acre tract of land that was up for sale at Depression prices. The land had been an old indigo plantation known as Fruitlands. Jones was intrigued immediately. As he later wrote: 'I had been told, of course, about the marvellous trees and plants, but I was still unprepared for the great bonus of beauty Fruitlands offered. Frankly, I was overwhelmed by the exciting possibilities of a golf course set in the midst of such a nursery.'

Fielding Wallace, an Augusta textile manufacturer, was assigned to buy the property, while Jones and Roberts chose Dr Alister MacKenzie, one of the world's leading golf architects, to design the course. Jones and MacKenzie worked well together. Jones was the adviser, MacKenzie the architect. Jones and MacKenzie also agreed that the course should offer

the greatest enjoyment for the greatest number of players. As Jones said: 'Our overall aim at the Augusta National was to provide a golf course of considerable natural beauty, relatively easy for the average golfer to play, and at the same time testing for the expert player striving to better par figures. We hoped to make bogeys easy if frankly sought, pars readily obtainable by standard good play, and birdies, except on the par fives, dearly bought.' Which is how it turned out.

Construction of the course was begun in the spring of 1931 and was completed in the fall of 1932. It was sometime during the second year of the club's existence that the idea for the Masters was born. Some of the club members, proud of their course and wishing to show it off, thought it might be possible to hold the US Open there. But the Open was, and still is, a June event, and after many conversations with the USGA, it was agreed that the project was not feasible since the course in June would not be playable.

Clifford Roberts suggested that the club hold its own tournament in the spring, one that would show off the course and at the same time give the local golf fans a chance to see the game's best players. Roberts convinced Jones that the tournament could be distinguished from others on the pro circuit by casting Jones as host and having him invite leading players and his friends. That invitational quality still remains, although in reality it was altered greatly after the first year. Jones received so much static about who was invited and who was not that a qualification system was set up, the qualifying players then being 'invited' to compete.

At first Jones declined to play in the tournament, but Roberts convinced him that it would be impolite to invite so many golfing friends to Augusta and not play himself. It was also the persuasive Roberts who coined the name 'Masters' for the tournament. Jones at first rejected it on the grounds that it was too presumptuous, but the name stuck.

That first Masters began on 22 March 1934. The final headline was: 'Augusta Golf Tourney Won by Horton Smith as Jones Finishes 13th.' 'I hope everyone enjoyed himself,' said Bobby Jones, 'and I hope you'll all be back next year.' They did come back the following year and they have returned every year since, save for the brief period during World War II. There are many who argue that the Masters has become the best tournament of the year. Certainly it is the most special and, with remarkable frequency, the most exciting.

Certainly, over the years, the acknowledged great players have won – as they invariably will on a course that is a good, fair test. Certainly, too, the Masters championships since the war have helped establish the pattern of golfing history. In 1949 the era of Hogan–Snead began, although Ben was at home in bed recovering from the automobile accident that nearly killed

*Sam Snead*

him. During the next six years Hogan and Snead were to win five times. Snead began it.

In 1951, after nine tries, Hogan finally won, as everyone knew he must. 'If I never win another tournament, I'll be satisfied,' he said after Bobby Jones had helped him into his Masters green jacket, although of course there would be more to come. But in 1954 Snead took the lead over Hogan, three Masters jackets to two, and although one would have hardly predicted it then, it was the last time either would win a major championship. The 1954 Masters was their last dance.

Four years later, the Age of Palmer in the Masters was born – and in 1960 it reached full maturity. It was not so much that Palmer won both the Masters and the US Open that year, it was how he won them, coming out of the pack at the final turn and barreling past the leaders. Two words gained new meaning in 1960 – 'army' and 'charge'. 'Army' was Palmer's gallery at any given tournament – 'Arnie's Army' – that whooping, encouraging, stampeding sea of people who came to watch their man perform heroics and were more often than not satisfied. And what Palmer did was 'charge'. As in cavalry. Four shots back and five to play. Easy. During this period of Palmer's career he was quoted as saying, 'I feel anytime I have to make a birdie, I can', and it seemed he was right.

By 1965 it was clear that the Masters was being dominated by Palmer, Jack Nicklaus and South Africa's Gary Player much in the fashion that Ben Hogan and Sam Snead had dominated it during the early fifties. It had been Palmer in 1960, Player the next, Palmer again, then Nicklaus, and finally Palmer in 1964. During that period Palmer also had a tie for second, as did Nicklaus, and Player had lost a play-off.

And now it was Nicklaus again – with a vengeance! In 1965 it was left to Bobby Jones to sum up Jack's performance. First he congratulated Palmer and Player, who tied for second at 280, a score that would have won all but five previous Masters. 'Palmer and Player played superbly,' said the old Master. 'As for Nicklaus, he plays a game with which I am not familiar.' And when, in 1966, Nicklaus won again it meant that for the first time in the history of the tournament, a Masters champion had successfully defended his title, thus posing officials with a problem. 'Cliff and I have discussed this situation,' Jones said at the victory ceremony. 'We have decided you will just have to put the green jacket on yourself.'

In the past nine years, only Art Wall, in 1959, had broken the tight circle formed by the Big Three. When everyone teed off in 1967, the only question was which one of the three would win it this time. How could anyone foretell that the Masters was about to enter a five-year period when none of them would win, when in fact the tournament would be dominated by the ordinary touring pro?

*Arnold Palmer*

In 1972, though, no one ever seriously challenged Jack Nicklaus as he led from start to finish. So many times in the past the tension has been almost unbearable as the leaders have gone through Amen Corner – the 11th, 12th and 13th – on Sunday afternoon. This time there was none, as Nicklaus held a five-stroke lead. He won by a comfortable three, thus giving him his fourth Masters title, tying him with his friendly rival, Palmer.

And, come 1974, after Tommy Aaron had won the previous year, no one surely seriously challenged the right of Gary Player to win his second Masters title. It had been a long time, thirteen years, since his first, but it was a reminder of the South African's fantastic resilience – and a reminder, too, of the Masters as a championship so often won by the world's greatest players.

## The USPGA Championship

Of the game's four major tournaments, the PGA Championship has fallen last on the annual schedule more often than not since a Philadelphia department store scion put up its first cash kitty – $2580 – just before World War I. This position has been symbolic of its stature among this premium quartet of tournaments through the years since the Professional Golfers' Association of America held its first Championship in 1916.

The tournament probably will continue to anchor these 'Big Four' on the schedule – and this is not all bad. Think of the attention and prestige it might have attracted in 1972 if Lee Trevino had not holed a chip shot on the 71st hole of the British Open. Jack Nicklaus could have been teeing off on August 3 at one of America's great courses – Oakland Hills – with three legs up on the never-attained Professional Grand Slam of Golf – the two Opens, Masters and PGA in a single season. The PGA already had its first ticket sell-out in history before Trevino beat Nicklaus at Muirfield, and defections were heavy among the news media planning to be in Detroit after the sports story of the year went out the window in July in Scotland.

But even given the boost of being part of the wondrous Grand Slam, and granting the efforts that today's PGA officials are putting forth to make a true classic of their championship, the tournament seems destined to remain at best a distant fourth in the eyes of the golfing public.

The irony of this is that today, after sundry changes, the PGA Championship now has overall the strongest competitive field of all, based on qualification and the inclusion of the top 60 money-winners on the US tour. It is, like the Opens and Masters, a four-day, four-round championship – and if ever the Grand Slam is achieved, this event will be the decisive setting. We shall see.

# 3 The courses

Arnold Palmer

# Carnoustie

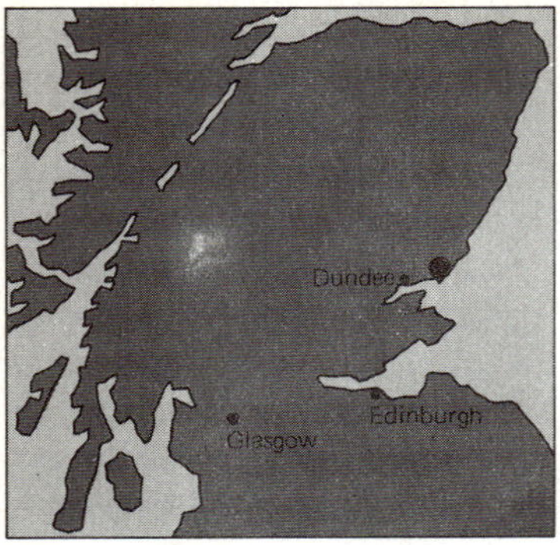


# British Open 1975

Apart from being the Open Championship venue for the fifth time in 1975, Carnoustie, in the Scottish county of Angus, just across the River Tay from St Andrews, has other claims to distinction. Its most recent measurement of 7042 yards makes it one of the longest championship courses in Britain and the best rounds recorded there in the British Open were of 68, by Ben Hogan (1953) and Billy Casper (1968). Leaving figures on one side, Carnoustie has earned a specially warm place in American golfing hearts, through the number of teaching professionals it has produced to carry the gospel abroad. Among them was Stewart Maiden, of whom the late Bobby Jones wrote: 'I picked up my game watching him play, unconsciously as a monkey and as imitatively. I grew up swinging so precisely like Stewart that an old friend of Stewart's mistook me for him.'

Golf in the immediate neighbourhood of the present course has been played since the 16th century, when the Register of Panmure for the year 1527 records that Sir Robert Maule, 'colarique' of nature and subject to 'suddane anger', 'exercisit the gowf' on the Barry Links, 'quhan (when) the wadsie (wager) was for drink'. By 1830 there were ten rudimentary holes on the course. It was reconstructed on land bought from the Earl of Dalhousie in 1842, still with ten holes, and extended to 18 by Old Tom Morris in 1872. According to *The Golfers' Handbook*, the first time a bookmaker shouted the odds at a golf tournament was at Carnoustie in 1898. James Braid redesigned the course in 1926, and his relatively short finish was changed to the present famous run for home in 1930. The final three holes have since been one of the toughest tests in world golf, as players attempt to keep out of the Barry Burn's ubiquitous water.

The links at Carnoustie are among the most windswept of any British seaside course. Both the courses, the Championship and Burnside, are public and four local clubs play over them.

**Hole 1** 406 yards Par 4

The green is set in a hollow, giving the hole its name, 'The Cup'. The Barry Burn makes its introduction, some seventy yards from the tee, but should be only a psychological hazard at this point. In the 1952 Scottish Amateur Championship, however, a player hooked three successive drives into the water, then told his partner he was finished and walked back to the clubhouse – probably the shortest championship appearance on record.

Drive — There are two new bunkers on the right of the fairway, at about 240 and 260 yards from the tee. Left centre of the very bumpy fairway is favoured for the best approach to the green. Black and white posts on the banks of the burn mark out of bounds to their left.

2nd Shot — Probably a 3-iron and fairly straightforward, so long as your drive has not gone too far to the right, where a jutting sandhill gives a blind shot to the green.

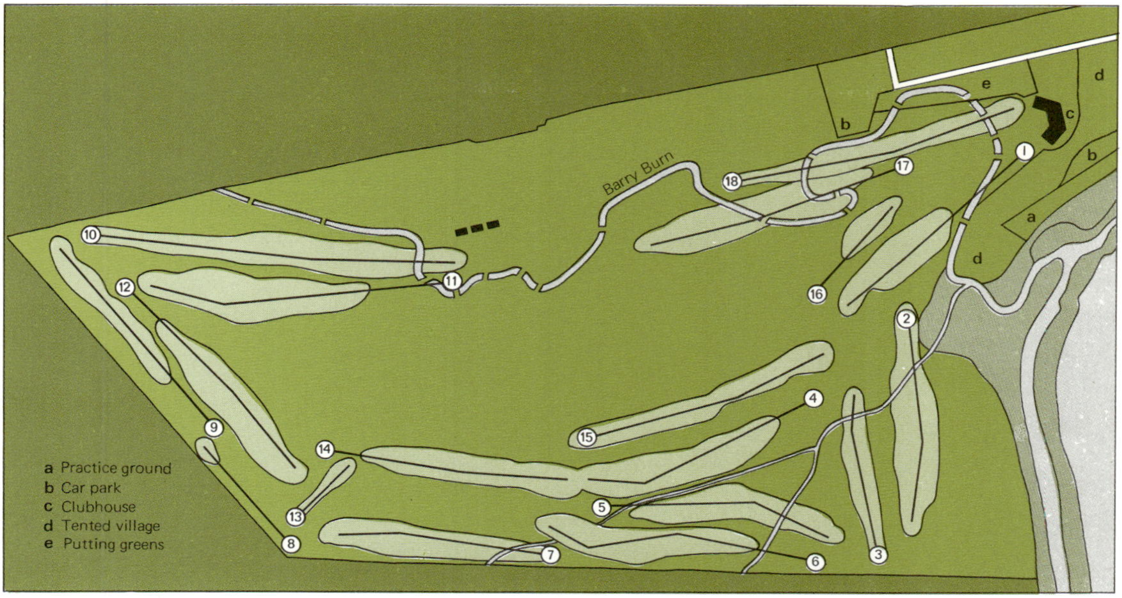


**Total length** 7042 yds
**Out** 3487 yds
**In** 3555 yds

**Hole 1**

**Hole 2** 441 yards Par 4

Known as 'Gulley' because the narrow fairway runs along a shallow valley between the sandhills. A feature is the controversial and dominating bunker put in by James Braid, at the centre of the fairway over 200 yards from the tee. The green was extended backwards some years ago on a slightly higher level than its front part and, when the flag is at the back, the out-of-bounds fence lies only a few yards behind it. A very demanding par-4.

Drive Again slightly left of centre, to avoid the Braid bunker.

2nd Shot Can be a wood if you are facing the unpredictable wind, and the green is guarded by bunkers on both sides.

**Hole 3** 348 yards Par 4

Named 'Jockie's Burn' – and the longer your tee shot, the greater the danger of landing in it, as it meanders across the fairway just in front of the green.

Drive With an iron from an elevated tee down to a fairly narrow fairway, with rough and a tree plantation on the left and more rough, with a line of hillocks, on the right. Keep short of the burn.

2nd Shot If your pitch to the gently sloping green is correct, there is a good chance of a birdie 3.

**Hole 4** 379 yards Par 4

'Hillocks', a plain, fairly flat hole played as a slight dogleg right.

Drive A ditch runs along the later part of the fairway, but this catches only badly-pulled drives and the main problem is to miss some well-placed, but visible bunkers on the right.

2nd Shot Absence of background to the large green, which is shared with the 14th hole, makes this a good test of distance judgment.

**Hole 5** 397 yards Par 4

Known as 'Brae' and the turning-point in Ben Hogan's Open victory of 1953. He was on a grass bank beside a bunker to the left rear of the green in his final round and seemed to be showing signs of faltering. He chipped in for a three and never looked back in a record round of 68. The hole is slightly dogleg right.

Drive Jockie's Burn crosses the fairway about 260 yards from the tee and most players keep short of it, though this can be tricky with a following wind.

2nd Shot Best approach is from the right of the fairway to the two-level raised green and complete accuracy is needed for par 4 to be achieved.

**Hole 6** 524 yards Par 5

'Long Hole' is the right name, as it is among the longest on Britain's Championship courses and some rate it the best. The true, old-fashioned three-shot approach, a rarity today. An out-of-bounds fence runs all along the left, Jockie's Burn and a lateral ditch slant across from the right and there are some well-placed big bunkers in the middle of the fairway.

Drive To carry Jockie's Burn – and one narrow line is 'Hogan's Alley', between the bunkers and the fence, though the margin for error is very small.

2nd Shot The approach to the green bends in from the left and you must beware the ditch jutting in from the right.

**Hole 2**

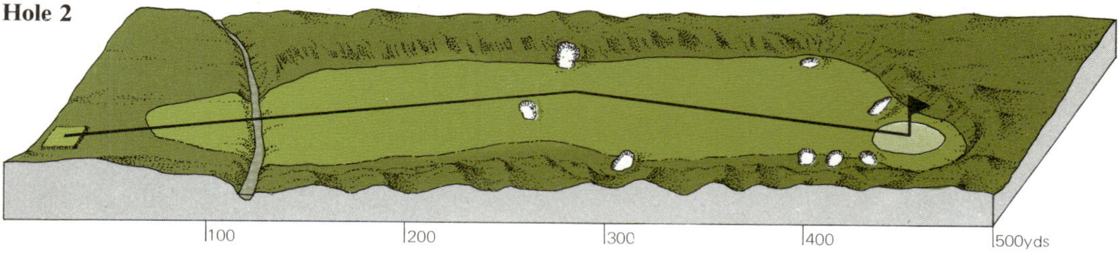


**Hole 3**

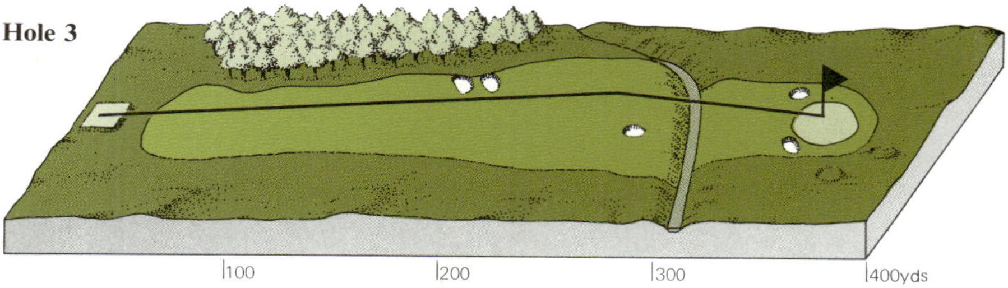


**Hole 4**

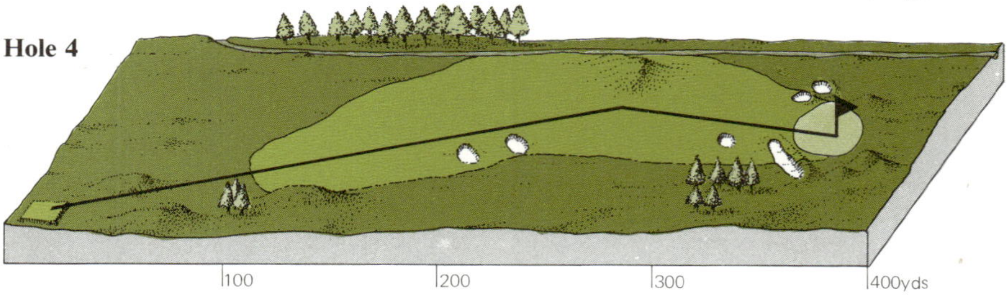


**Hole 5**

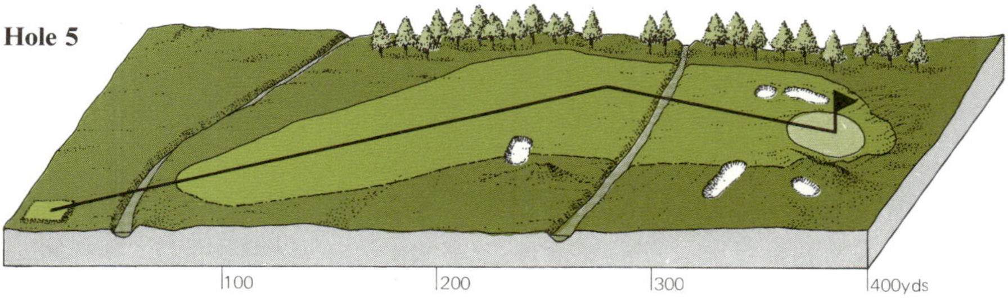


**Hole 6**

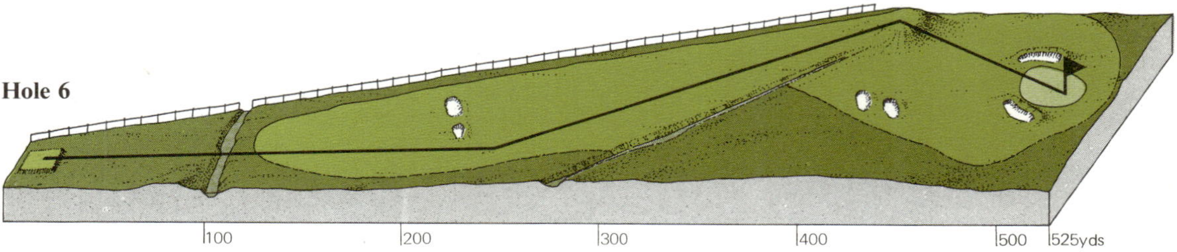

**Hole 7** 397 yards Par 4

'Plantation' takes its name from the trees on the right, with the same out-of-bounds fence as on the previous hole running all along the left. Fairly straightforward and a reasonable chance to birdie.

Drive Avoid the strategically placed bunkers at about 200 and 280 yards from the tee.

2nd Shot The down-sloping green is guarded by two bunkers at the front.

**Hole 8** 174 yards Par 3

First of Carnoustie's three short holes, at right angles to the 7th and the start of the western side of the course. The out-of-bounds fence continues along the left and it is all too easy to hook over it. The large green is very closely guarded by bunkers on either side.

**Hole 9** 421 yards Par 4

Called the 'Railway', because the line runs back of the green. Still out-of-bounds on the left, in or over the trench indicated by black and white posts.

Drive Apart from the out-of-bounds, you must avoid bunkers and heathery rough on both sides.

2nd Shot Fairly straightforward, but the lateral ditch on the right must be avoided.

**Hole 10** 453 yards Par 4

Oddly named 'South America' after an old Scotsman who intended to emigrate there in the dim and distant past. Some farewell drams sapped his intentions and he got only as far as the green on this hole and went to sleep. Or so the story says. The picturesque green is girdled with trees, with the ubiquitous Barry Burn looping in front.

Drive Steer safely between a crop of bunkers on the right and one to the left, where there is considerable rough.

2nd Shot Over the burn and watch out for the two bunkers front left of the green.

**Hole 11** 372 yards Par 4

'Dyke' is a comparatively easy four with straight hitting, but usually plays longer than its 372 yards because it is almost always against the wind.

Drive Main dangers are the three big bunkers on the right.

2nd Shot Should be perfectly simple, between the bunkers guarding the green to left and right.

**Hole 12** 478 yards Par 5

'Southward Ho', because that is its direction, and in some ways the hardest hole on the course, with dangers everywhere.

Drive Watch for the lateral ditch on the right, heathery rough on both sides of the fairway and the two bunkers at about driving length.

2nd Shot The approach to the green is flanked by steep, bunker-set mounds.

**Hole 7**

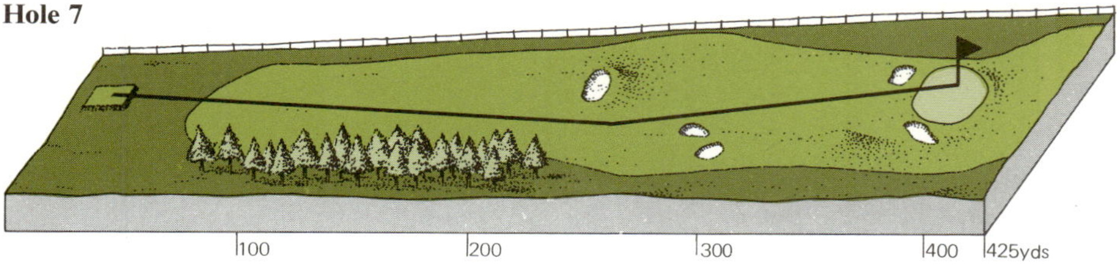


**Hole 8**

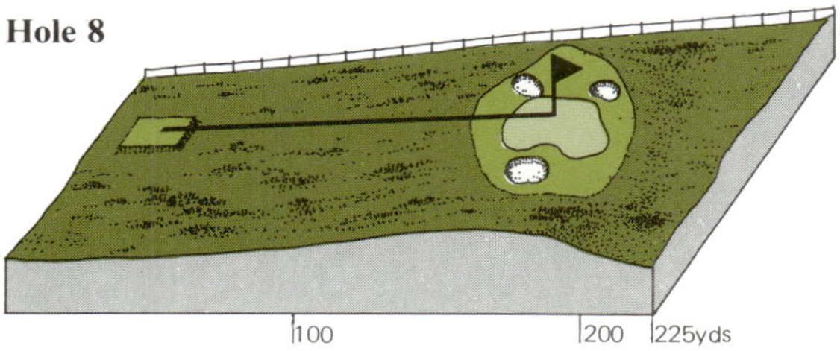


**Hole 9**

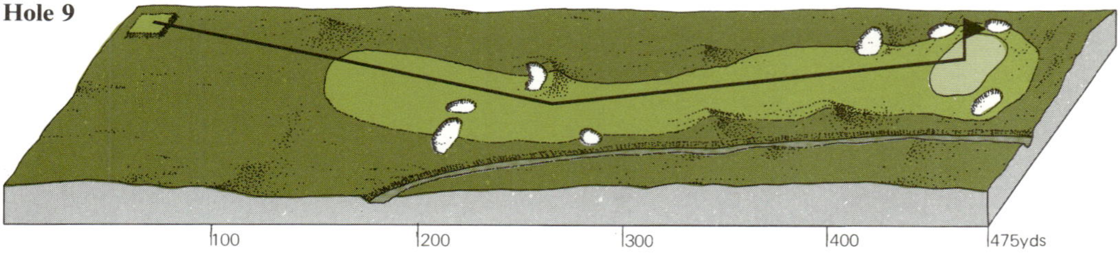


**Hole 10**

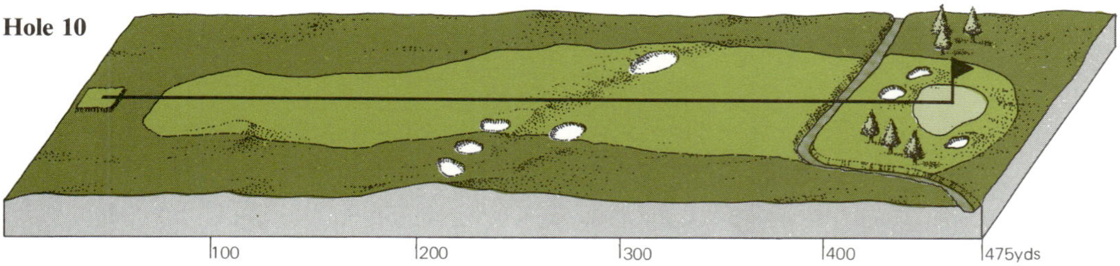


**Hole 11**

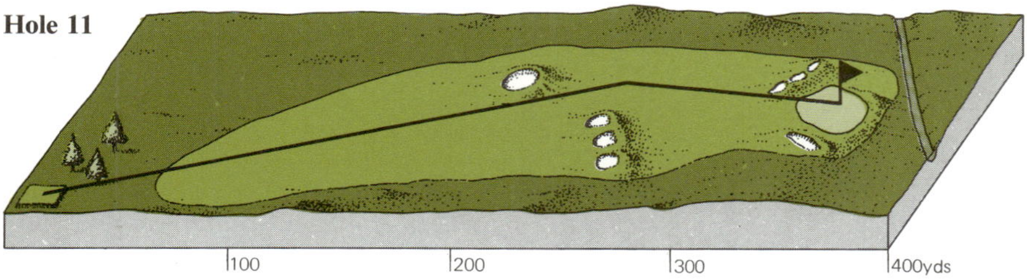


**Hole 12**

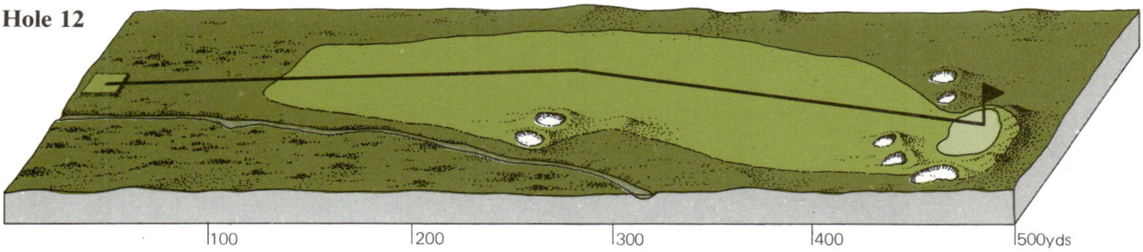

**Hole 13** 166 yards Par 3

'Whins' is the second short hole and it generally plays downwind. The opening to the green is protected by bunkers which encroach on the putting surface. The green slopes from the back-right.

**Hole 14** 488 yards Par 5

Called 'Spectacles', because of the big twin bunkers in the face of the ridge running across the fairway some 60 yards short of the green, which is shared with the 4th hole. The hole is played as a slight dogleg left. Out-of-bounds on the left is indicated by black and white posts.

Drive A good, solid hit to a point midway between bunkers on the left and right.

2nd Shot Played blind, because of the ridge, which must be carried.

**Hole 15** 461 yards Par 4

'Lucky Slap'. Another slight dogleg left.

Drive Rather to the right, because a pull may land you in a deep valley from which the flag cannot be seen.

2nd Shot Accuracy essential, through a bottleneck with a bunker on each side to the green in a hollow.

**Hole 16** 235 yards Par 3

Called 'Barry Burn' and the start to one of the most notoriously testing finishes in golf. The burn itself bends in near the green, but is away to the left and should cause trouble only if your drive is badly pulled. The length makes this a severe one-shotter and the narrow, raised green is guarded by bunkers. It is sometimes impossible to reach the green with a driver, but the danger when playing downwind will be to stay on it, not to reach it. One of the truly great short holes.

**Hole 17** 454 yards Par 4

One of the most famous holes in championship golf, with the threat of the Barry Burn coming into its own, as it threads its way along, looping back towards the tee and then away again to form 'The Island'.

Drive Risk trying to carry the far loop of the burn and you may well land right in it. The shot has to be aimed accurately on to the island of fairway and, downwind, you cannot hit full out.

2nd Shot A very long one needed to reach the green and take care not to fade into the three bunkers trapping the green to the right.

**Hole 18** 448 yards Par 4

'Home'. This has been shortened from its previous 510 yard par 5. The burn crosses the fairway, then flanks it to the left, waiting to receive hooked drives, and there is also an out-of-bounds fence on this side. The flowerbed behind the 1st tee and 18th green is also out-of-bounds.

Drive Carrying the backward loop of the burn and to the centre of the fairway, with three lateral bunkers to the right.

2nd Shot Unless the wind is hard behind, you must decide whether to attempt to carry the burn, which again crosses the fairway some 20 yards short of the green and is some 25 feet wide.

**Hole 13**

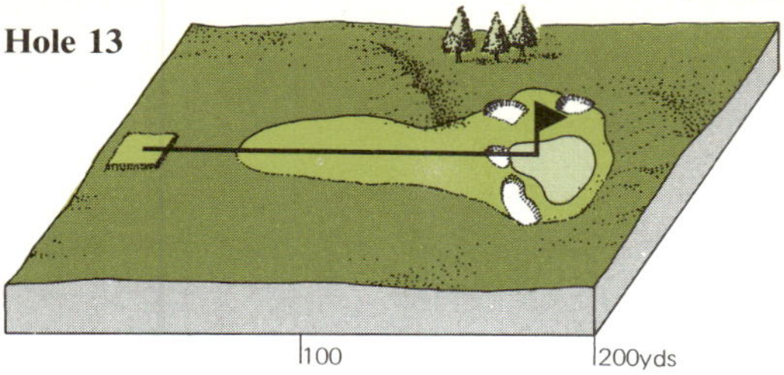


**Hole 14**

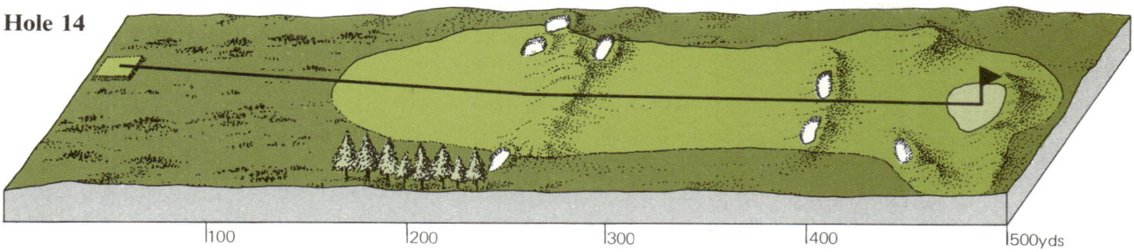


**Hole 15**

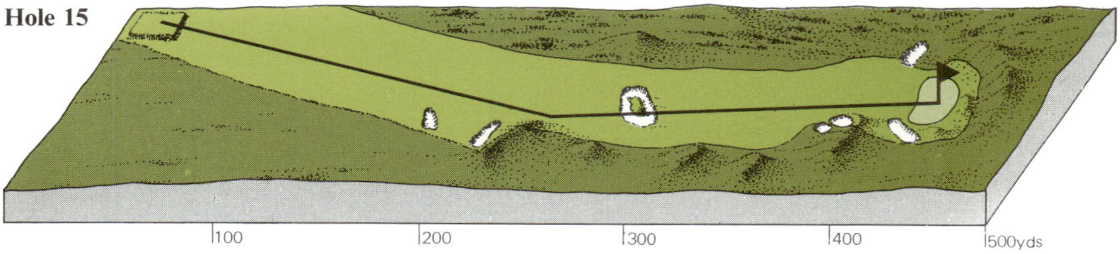


**Hole 16**

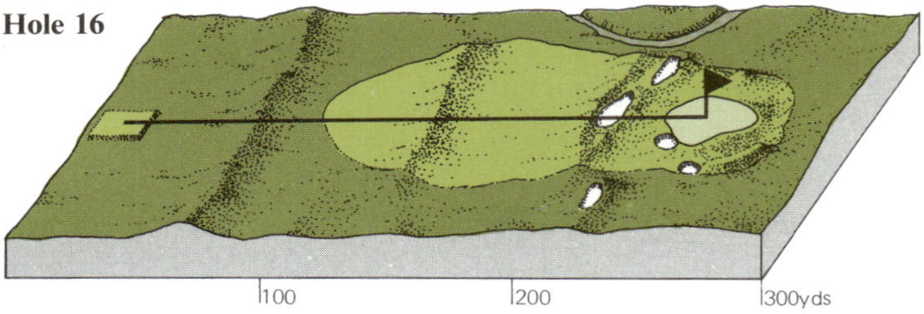


**Hole 17**

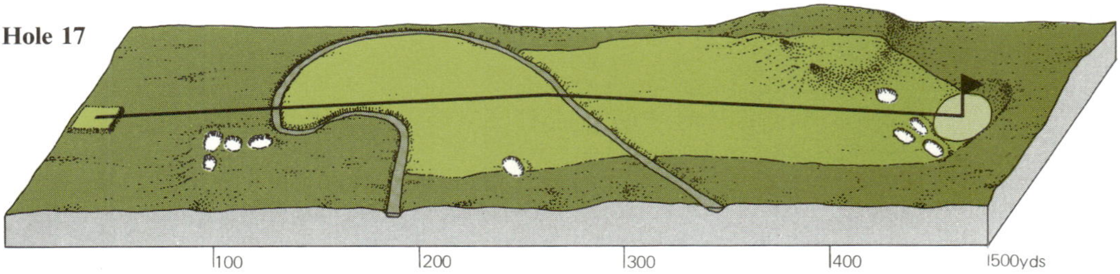


**Hole 18**

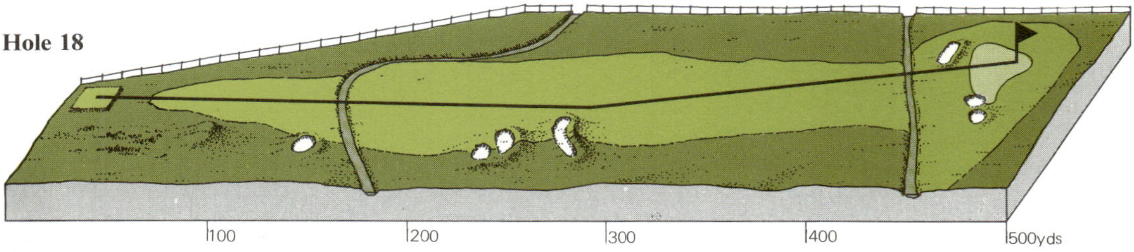

# Royal Birkdale

# British Open 1976

Birkdale, given the 'Royal' accolade in 1951, will stage its fifth Open Championship in 1976. It joined the select group of courses at which Britain's premier golf event is held in 1940, but did not get its first Open Championship until 1954. This might suggest that Birkdale is of relatively recent origin as a club and the present buildings do, in fact, date from only 1935, with extensions added in 1961. But Birkdale's history stretches back to 1889, the year when Willie Park junior won the second of his Open titles up at Musselburgh and in which eight local golfers rented a plot of land at Southport for £5 a year and laid nine holes on it. Membership subscriptions were set at a guinea a year (five shillings for ladies) and the club rooms in a nearby hotel cost a yearly sum of £3.

Eight years after its formation, the club moved to the present site among the Lancashire sandhills to the south of Southport and the number of holes was increased to 18. Countless changes and improvements have been made since then and the present course, 'as modern as supersonic planes' in Peter Thomson's words – he should know, having won two Open Championships there – ranks among the finest in the British Isles.

Not all the alterations have been popular. Before the 1971 Open the previously fearsome bunkers were completely refaced, earning a caustic comment from Jack Nicklaus: 'I liked the course the way it used to be, because it eliminated ninety per cent of the field, the players who did not have the game to handle it.'

For facilities and organisation, however, Birkdale has long been beyond reproach. Apart from four Open Championships, it has twice staged the Ryder Cup and such other international events as the unhappily now defunct Carling World Open, in 1966, and the Alcan two years later.

**Hole 1** 493 yards Par 5

A left-hand dogleg, with the wind – usually from the left – always liable to provide additional trouble, as on all seaside courses. Sometimes no one can get up in two; at others, it is a drive and an iron.

Drive — Between a big mound on the left and the out-of-bounds fence on the right, with rough scrub on both sides. Mounds jutting in from left and right can obscure the flag, so you want to be fairly close to the bunker on the left.

2nd Shot — A 3-iron or wood and you need to clear the mound jutting in from the right, just short of the green, with two bunkers nestling behind it to catch faded shots. Another bunker guards the left and there are various hollows behind and round the green.

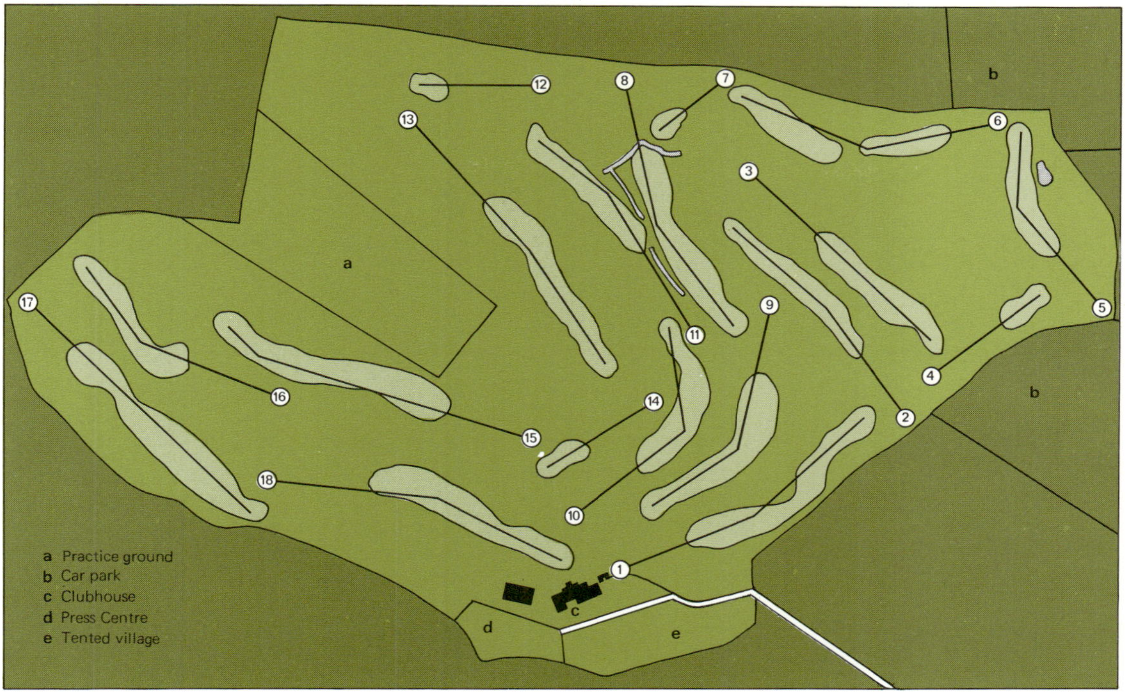


**Total length** 7080 yards
**Out** 3406 yards
**In** 3674 yards

**Hole 1**

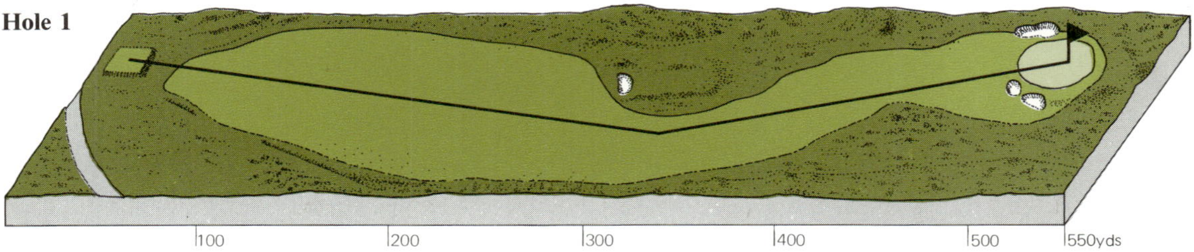

**Hole 2** 427 yards Par 4

Needs to be played hard, with no chance to relax. It runs virtually at right angles to the first hole and many consider it one of Birkdale's best par-4s. One of its attractions is the siting of the green, backed by a clump of dwarf pines growing on the sandhills, with bunkers at either side.

Drive — Down the middle of the fairway – and beware the sandy bank at drive length on the left.

2nd Shot — Over a big, old-fashioned cross-bunker 30 yards short of the green, with a 4- or 5-iron.

**Hole 3** 416 yards Par 4

Parallel to the second, but played in the opposite direction, with the prevailing wind. Trouble and scrub on both sides of the fairway, with two bunkers on the right.

Drive — Preferably over to the left, to open up the fairly narrow entry to the green and avoid playing blind over the big sandhill jutting in from the right. A bunker guards the front of the green on the left.

2nd Shot — Ideally an easy 9-iron, but even Arnold Palmer has often found this one troublesome and gone into the rough at the back of the green.

**Hole 4** 212 yards Par 3

Not rated the best of Birkdale's par-3s. You climb up steps to an elevated tee among the sandhills and play down on to a fairly big green, surrounded by humps and bunkers. The wind tends to push you out to the right and it is better to be long than short, because it is easier to recover from behind the green than from the ring of bunkers guarding its front. Boldness pays.

**Hole 5** 358 yards Par 4

A dogleg right nowadays, since it was altered to avoid a wet fairway, and still considered Birkdale's easiest par-4 by some players.

Drive — Straight down the middle of the fairway, with no bunkers to worry about, but nasty rough on both sides.

2nd Shot — The green is almost surrounded by bunkers and if your iron is short, you land in one of them; too long and you are in the rough, but it must be firmly hit.

**Hole 6** 473 yards Par 4

Tom Scott has called it the 'perfect golf hole, calling for both length and judgment'. Like many of the other holes it is played along a valley: this is bisected by a ridge and cross-bunker, from which point the hole bends right.

Drive — If you clear the ridge, there is a fairly simple pitch to the armchair green, but this takes considerable courage. A short drive leaves you with a blind shot to the green, which has formidable bunkers at each of its front corners.

2nd Shot — Not easy to get up in two: Arnold Palmer did not once manage it when winning the 1961 Open.

**Hole 2**

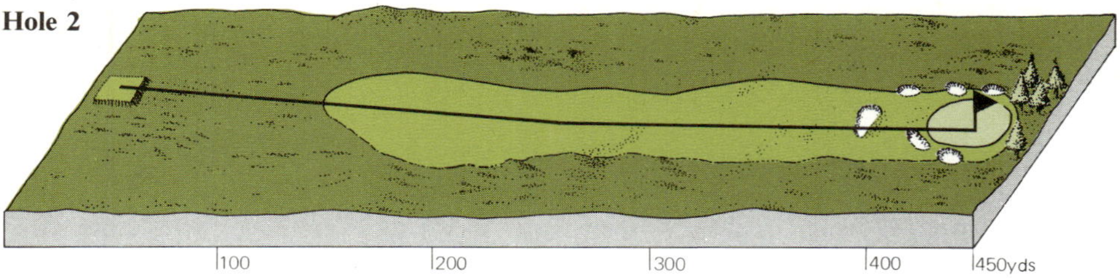


**Hole 3**

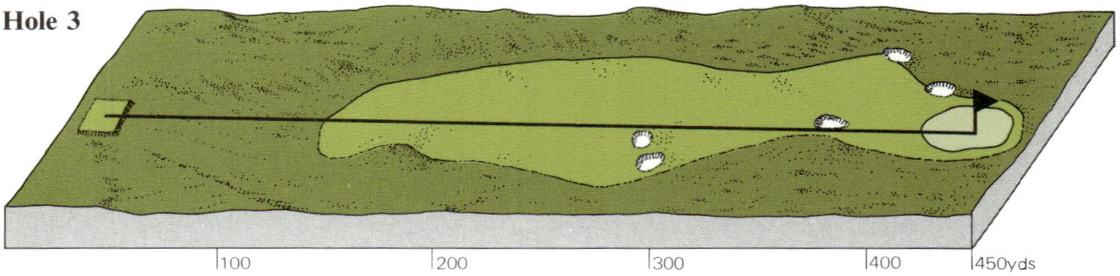


**Hole 4**

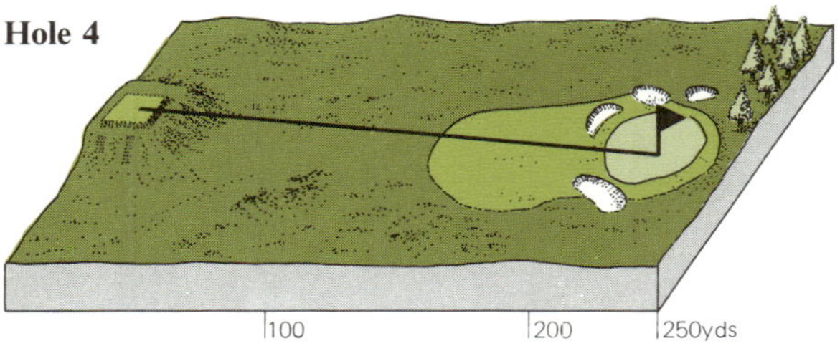


**Hole 5**

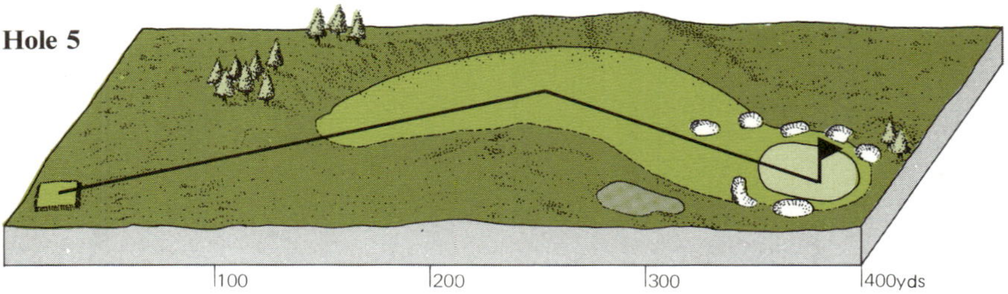


**Hole 6**

**Hole 7** 158 yards Par 3
Shortest hole on the course and, like the fourth, played from a high tee among the sand dunes. It can be difficult to judge the distance in windy conditions. Played over rough to a green well protected by five bunkers. A 7- or 8-iron favoured.

**Hole 8** 459 yards Par 4
Another elevated tee back in the sandhills. Played as a slight dogleg left, with the fairway narrowing at driving distance. Doug Sanders once took three shots to get out of one of the right-hand bunkers, which stand in echelon awaiting the faded drive.

Drive: Fatal to attempt to shorten the hole by driving left, as the banking on that side offers no opening to the green. Keep right, but beware of those bunkers. The tee shot is all-important.

2nd Shot: Turn slightly left, for a long straight 7- or 8-iron to a green which has high sandhills and bunkers on either side.

**Hole 9** 410 yards Par 4
A right-hand dogleg, with the narrow fairway out of sight from the tee. One of Birkdale's best holes.

Drive: Over the marker, probably with an iron. You must miss a bunker and rough on the right and the leftward slope can take you into more rough scrub on the other side. An accurately placed shot will reach a plateau on the fairway, before it dips into a slight valley.

2nd Shot: A demanding pitch with a 3-, 4- or 5-iron to the elevated green. The ball must hold, as a deep slope over the back can involve a difficult return.

**Hole 10** 393 yards Par 4
Not a long hole, but difficult to reach the green in two. This sharp, left-hand dogleg starts the second loop at Birkdale.

Drive: Beware of hooking, because of the scrub-covered mound jutting in to make the dogleg.

2nd Shot: Needs to be precise, probably with a 7-iron, to avoid a deep bunker to the right of the sand-encircled green.

**Hole 11** 412 yards Par 4
From a high tee way back in the sandhills.

Drive: The wind usually blows straight at you; a change in direction could make the bunkers on the right a danger. Aim a shade to the right.

2nd Shot: A 5- or 6-iron for this very tight shot, over a cross-bunker to what is possibly the course's most difficult green. This narrows towards the back-right, where the hole is likely to be cut; there is a deep bunker on the left, trouble in the slope of tufty grass, and mounds all around.

**Hole 12** 190 yards Par 3
This comparatively new hole is the nearest to the sea and out of sight from the rest of the course. An accurate 3- or 4-iron over rough to a small patch of fairway, with two bunkers on each side, sloping up to the front of the green. The shot needs to be hit well up and to pitch on the green, which has scrub-covered sandhills towering at either side and the ground falling steeply away over a bank at the back.

**Hole 7**

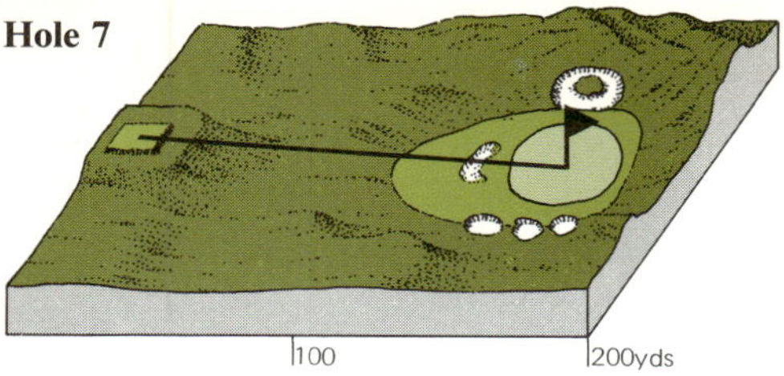


**Hole 8**

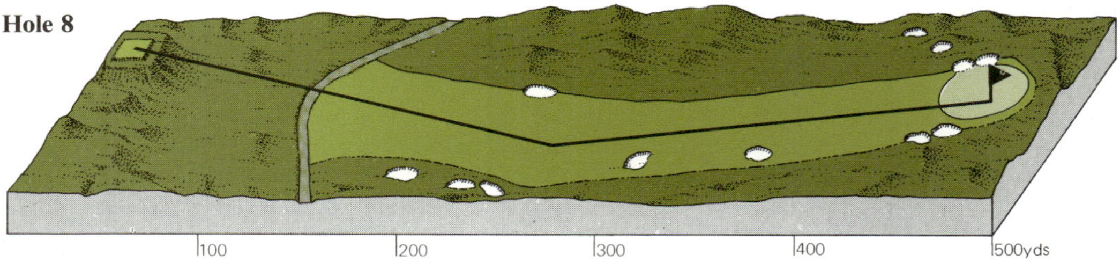


**Hole 9**

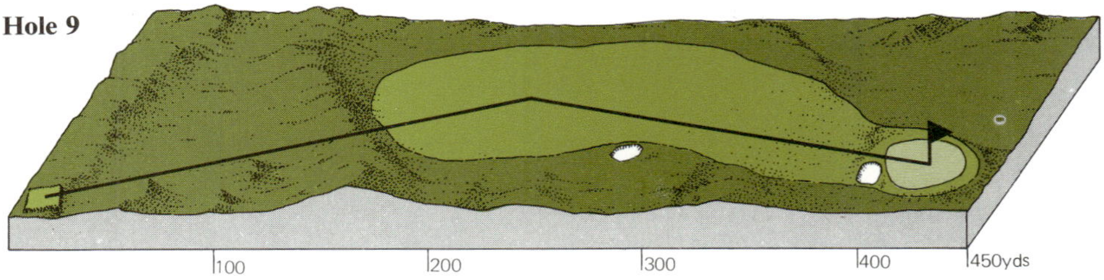


**Hole 10**

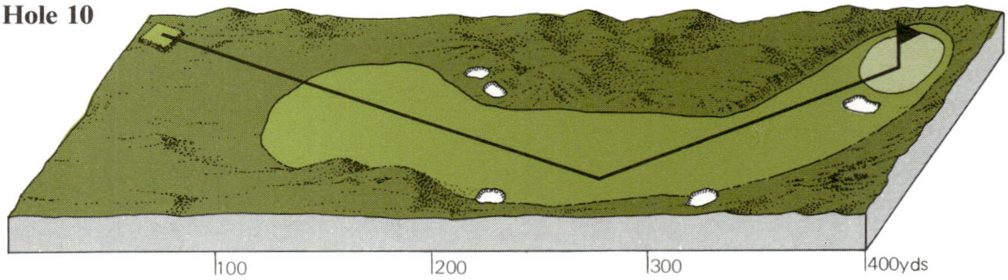


**Hole 11**

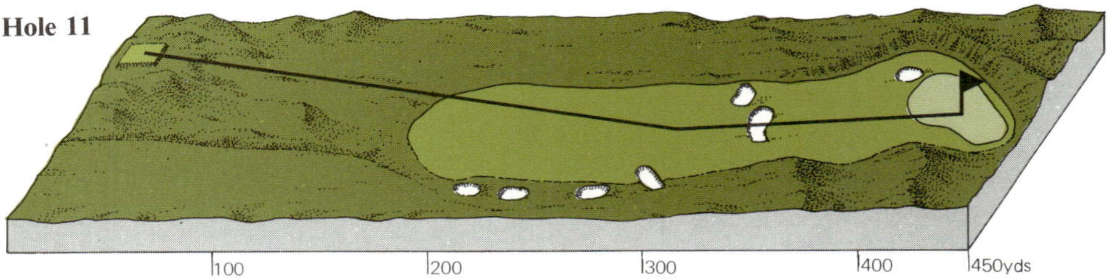


**Hole 12**

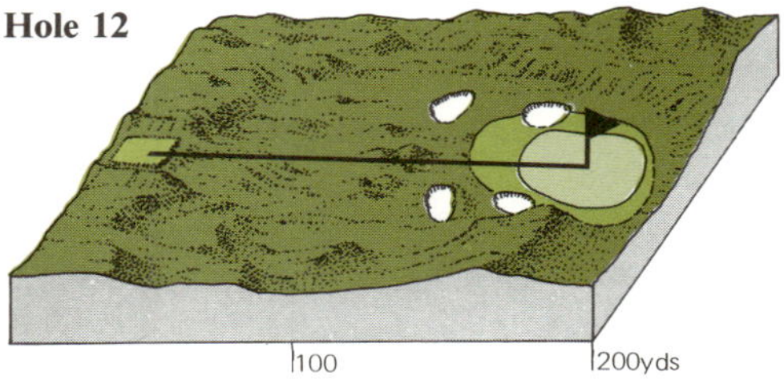

**Hole 13** 517 yards Par 5
Nearly all the trouble here is on the left, where the wind can take you into a ditch, bunkers and some tremendous rough.
Drive A good tee shot, slightly to the right, is the secret of this hole.
2nd Shot Fairly long, to a picturesque green, set in a hollow in the scrub-covered dunes, with bunkers on both sides.

**Hole 14** 202 yards Par 3
The longest of Birkdale's four short holes. A high tee and your shot must be on the large green to get par, as its undulations make a single putt very difficult. The green is practically surrounded by bunkers, with a particularly deep, straight-faced one to the left.

**Hole 15** 536 yards Par 5
Into the prevailing wind and possibly *plays* as the longest hole in Britain. Very few players can reach the green in two. In the 1937 Amateur Championship, James Bruen's drive bounced only one yard, then he hit the ball on to the green with a spoon.
Drive Up the middle of the fairway, avoiding the bunkers on the left, with length all-important to open up the green.
2nd Shot On a line left of the pin, to avoid a rash of bunkers across the fairway. This is usually followed by a pitch to the green – and it takes a poor third shot to land in the bunkers at the green's front corners.

**Hole 16** 401 yards Par 4
A plaque to the right of the fairway commemorates the second shot that won Arnold Palmer the 1961 Open, a 6-iron from deep rough on the right of the fairway straight on to the green.
Drive Needs tremendous carry over sandhills and scrub to the middle of the fairway for a good approach to the green from the dogleg right.
2nd Shot Has to carry bunkers to a raised plateau green, where it is difficult to land and stay. Bunkers on both sides of the green.

**Hole 17** 510 yards Par 5
Turns downwind in prevailing conditions and is difficult to drive. Another 1961 memory for Palmer here: he was penalised to his intense annoyance, after the wind had moved his ball several inches in the large bunker to the front right of the green, and made seven.
Drive Between two big sandhills jutting into the fairway, which is quite narrow.
2nd Shot A long one, over the flat fairway to a flat green backed by sandhills and willow scrub and well guarded by bunkers.

**Hole 18** 513 yards Par 5
The famous last hole, where Mr Lu's difficult second shot felled a woman spectator in the final round of the 1971 Open, but he still birdied, to finish a stroke behind Lee Trevino.
Drive The wind tends to push the ball out towards the dangerous rough on the right.
2nd Shot A 3-wood or 4-iron and you must avoid three infamous bunkers guarding the green.

Hole 13

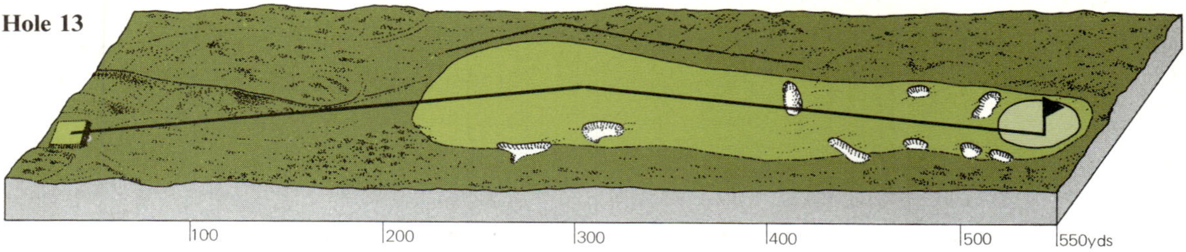


Hole 14

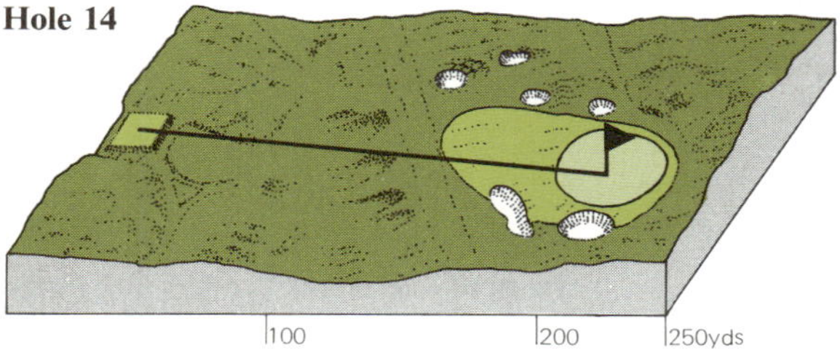


Hole 15

Hole 16

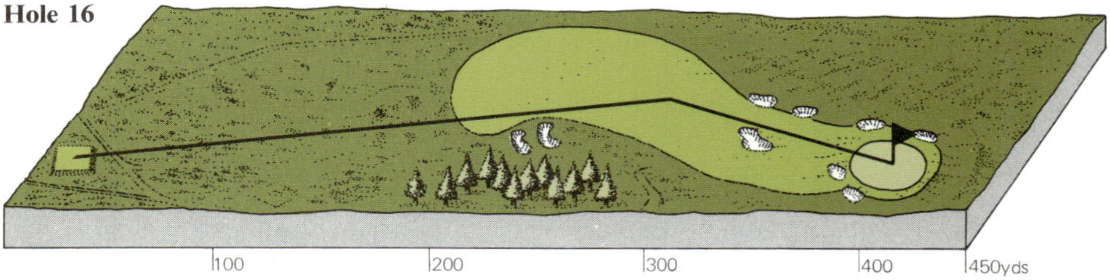


Hole 17

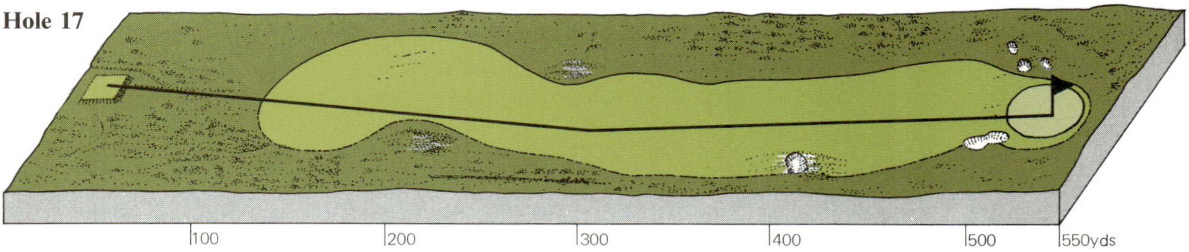


Hole 18

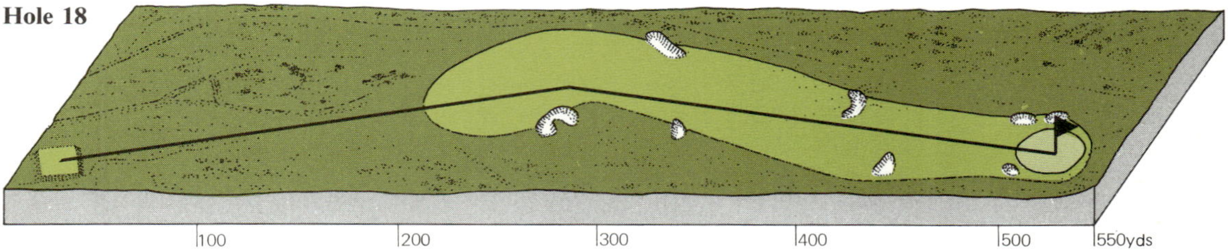

# Turnberry

## Double Diamond 1975

## British Open 1977

Turnberry, in Ayrshire on Scotland's West coast, has two courses attached to its British Transport hotel: the Ailsa, where major championships are held, and the easier Arran. Both take their names from islands: Ailsa Craig, a hump of granite not far offshore, and the Glasgow holiday 'lung' of Arran, a great mass to the north-west in the Firth of Clyde.

Golf was first played at Turnberry in 1902 and the British Women's Championship went there for the first of many times in 1912. During the Second World War the two courses became an airfield, but the flattening of the ground that this involved happily left Ailsa's sand dunes intact, providing some natural features as the basis of its reconstruction, by golf architect Mackenzie Ross. It was initiated as a championship course for men in 1954, with the Scottish PGA's title event, won in that year – and for the fifth of eight times – by John Panton.

Since then, the Match Play Championship, the Amateur Championship, the Walker Cup, the Home Internationals and many other important events have been held at Turnberry, whose 9th hole on the Ailsa Course, Bruce's Castle, is one of the most scenically beautiful and impressive of any in Britain. Ailsa staged the John Player Classic in 1972–3 and the Double Diamond will be played there in 1975, with the British Open coming to the course for the first time in 1977.

**Hole 1** 361 yards Par 4

'Ailsa Craig', named after the pile of granite out to sea, from which most of the world's curling stones are made. No great problems in this dogleg right. The prevailing wind is against you and slightly from the right.

Drive: Slightly left of the three bunkers on the right in the dogleg, the second two having been added because people began carrying the first. Brian Huggett started his 7-under-par record round of 64, in the 1972 John Player Classic, by carrying all three in a birdie 3.

2nd Shot: A straightforward mid-iron to the green.

**Hole 2** 426 yards Par 4

'Mak Siccar' is in the opposite direction and again a reasonably straightforward par-4 dogleg left.

Drive: Plenty of room for your shot from a tee against the fence.

2nd Shot: Slightly right of the two bunkers short of the green, with the fairway running away left.

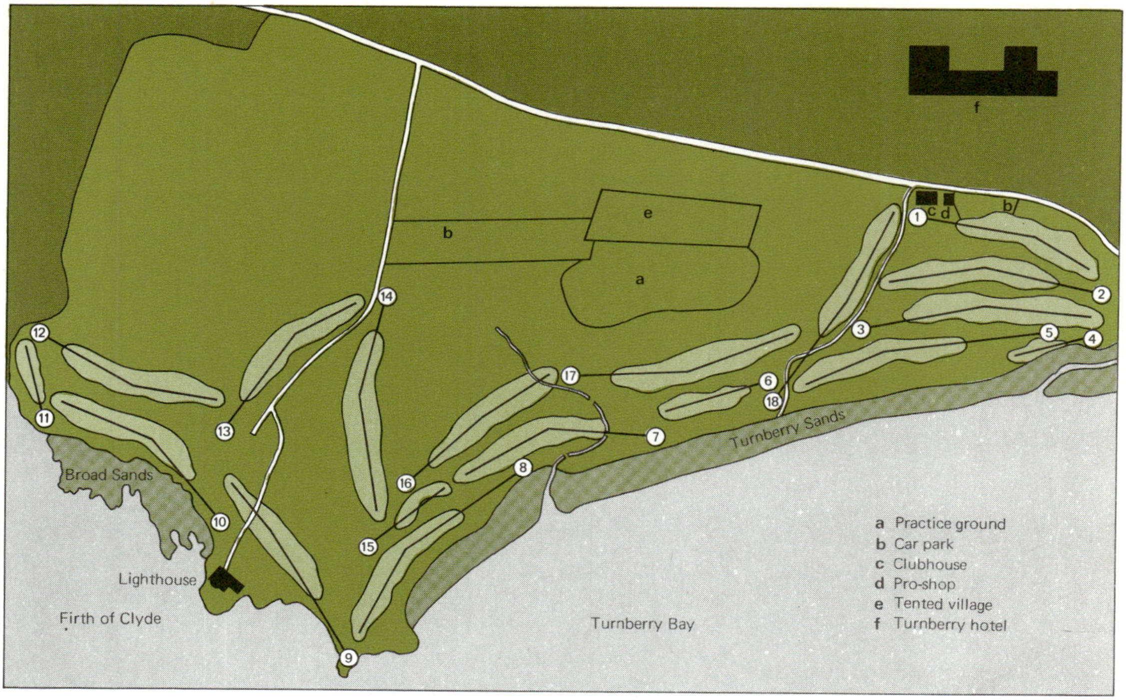


**Total length** 6936 yards
**Out** 3542 yards
**In** 3394 yards

**Hole 1**

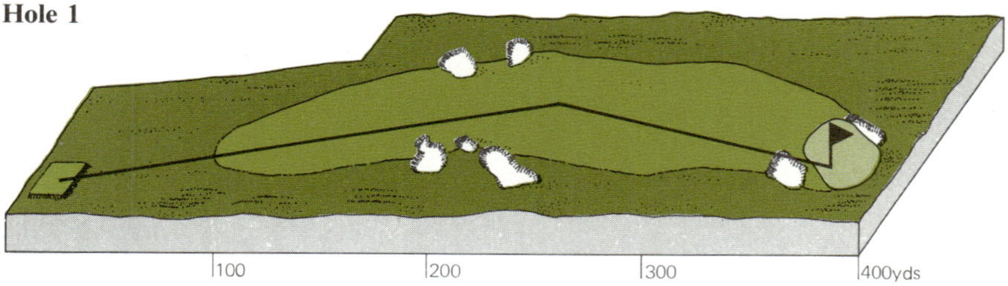


**Hole 2**

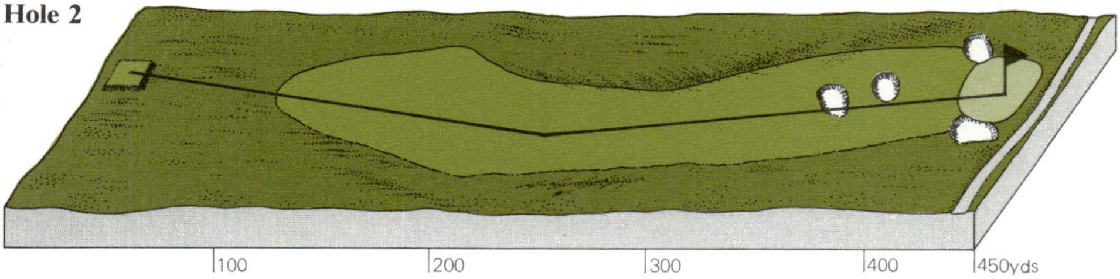

**Hole 3** 467 yards Par 4

'Blaw Wearie'. A fine two-shotter, often against the wind, which can make even hitting the fairway difficult.

Drive — Keep left. There are no bunkers along the fairway, but some rough and dips on the right.

2nd Shot — The sunken green is guarded by unseen traps right and left, and a long carry is needed to the heart of the green.

**Hole 4** 168 yards Par 3

'Woe-be-Tide' is aptly named: off to the left and you are in trouble on the beach, which runs all along this side. There is a very deep pit short-right of the elevated green and this tends to make it look closer than it really is. Too far right and you can be left with an awkward chip off the bank. A 6-iron is recommended.

**Hole 5** 482 yards Par 5

'Fin' me oot' is first of the par-5s, with a far-back tee. The fairly narrow fairway is guarded left by two bunkers, and there are ridged dunes on both sides of the valley.

Drive — Aim right to get safely past the two bunkers and far enough to open the green clear of another guarding it front-left.

2nd Shot — Dogleg half-left to the green set in a hollow, with two bunkers on its right – and probably hardest to find on the course.

**Hole 6** 242 yards Par 3

'Tappie Toorie' has a high tee and fairly high green. The drive carries a big dip and beware a trap on the left. The fast, difficult green slopes from back to front, heavily guarded by bunkers, with the huge one on the right particularly menacing to faded shots. Surely Turnberry's hardest par.

**Hole 7** 520 yards Par 5

'Roon the Ben' – 'Round the Bend' to Sassenachs – is Turnberry's longest hole and its name can be attributed either to its being a sharp dogleg left, or to the frame of mind of hookers into the tangle of gorse and brambles.

Drive — Quite a big carry for the ordinary player and as far down the straight fairway as you can get, aiming to the right of a big trap from a tee high on the dunes.

2nd Shot — Watch for the menacing trap, which caught Peter Townsend in 1972, and the deep pit short-left. The green is not very big.

**Hole 3**

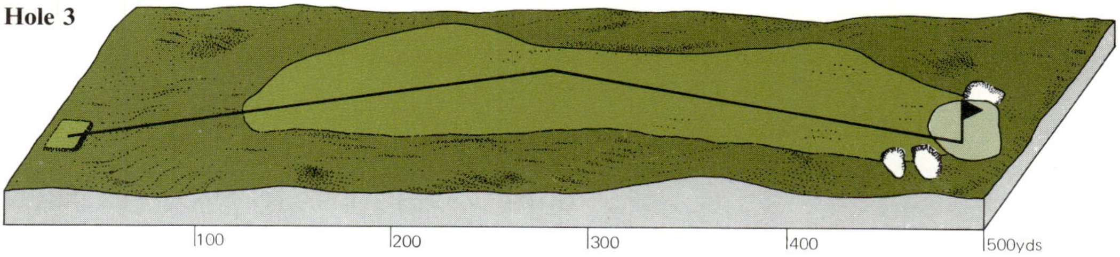


**Hole 4**

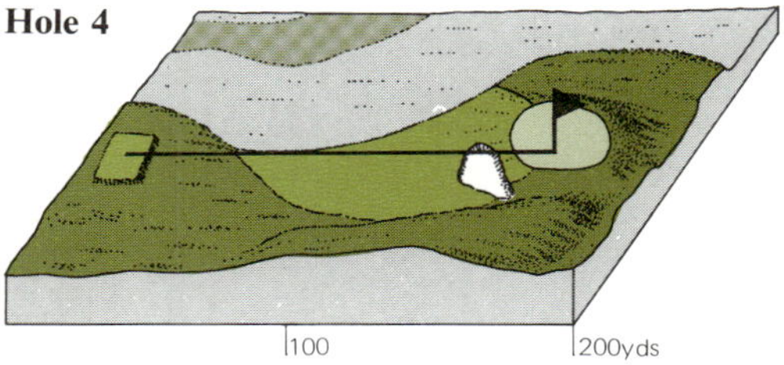


**Hole 5**

**Hole 6**

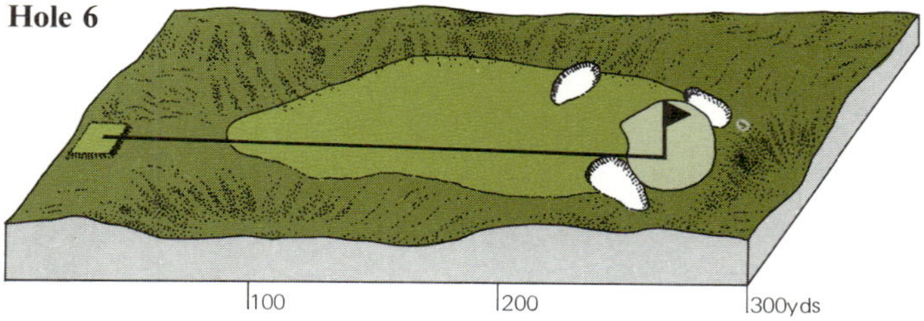


**Hole 7**

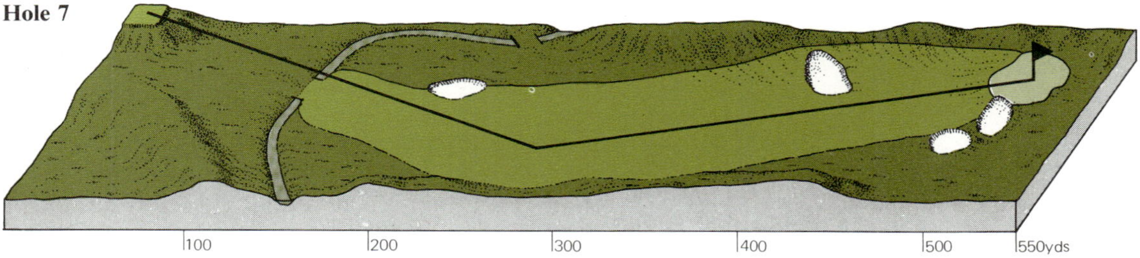

**Hole 8** 427 yards Par 4

'Goat Fell' is a splendid driving hole, still following the line of the shore, with the tee almost on it.

Drive The dangerous right-hand bunker, jutting into the fairway, narrows your landing area and the drive must be drawn. The fairway slopes from left to right.

2nd Shot A long iron to the elevated two-terrace green, with a fast surface and vicious bunkers on either side forming a fairly difficult target.

**Hole 9** 449 yards Par 4

'Bruce's Castle', unquestionably one of Britain's most spectacular holes, with the tee jutting out on a spit of land above the rocks, and the lighthouse in front of you to the left.

Drive The line is across the water and blind over a cairn of stones on the horizon – a carry of some 215 yards.

2nd Shot Turn slightly left and go for the narrow, unguarded green, which throws the shot off right or left and you can end up in gorse bushes.

**Hole 10** 453 yards Par 4

'Dinna Fouter' on the turn for home is another attractive hole, with the chance to open your shoulders from a distant tee high among the bushes.

Drive Over a carry of rocks and scrub to a fairly wide fairway and not quite so demanding as the last hole.

2nd Shot Downhill with a mid-iron, to clear a huge cross-bunker in front of the green, which can seem nearer than it really is and slopes downwards.

**Hole 11** 178 yards Par 3

'Maidens'. From an elevated tee beside the beach and nearly always downwind to a green guarded by frontal and right-hand bunkers. The spacious green is slightly elevated and wind can make putting difficult.

**Hole 12** 390 yards Par 4

After following the shoreline from hole 4, you now turn away from it. The hole takes its name, 'Monument', from the RAF memorial standing above the green to the right and is played against the prevailing wind.

Drive Three big traps in the left of the fairway force you to the right, but if you go too far, bunkers on that side of the green will give you a tricky approach.

2nd Shot About a 6-iron to clear the front-of-green traps. The raised green slopes away to the left.

**Hole 8**

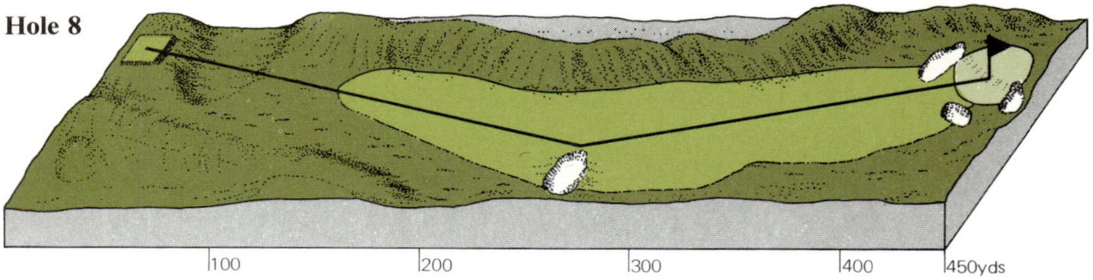


**Hole 9**

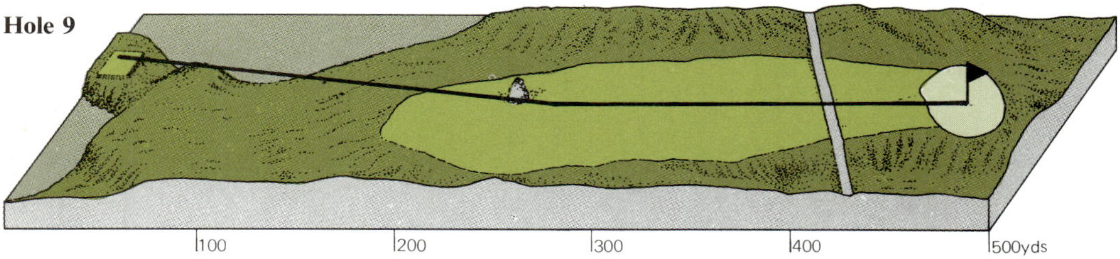


**Hole 10**

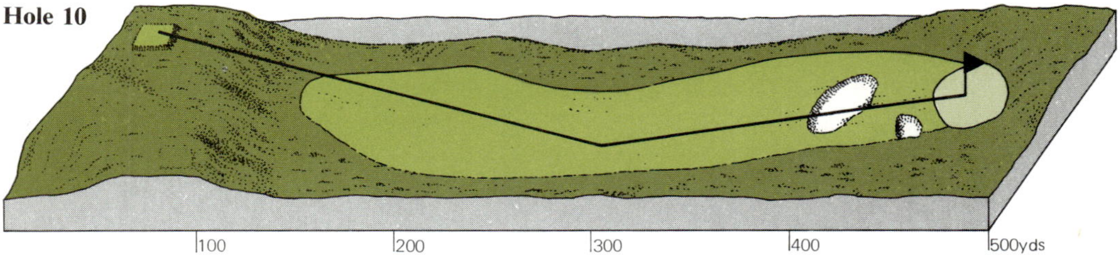


**Hole 11**

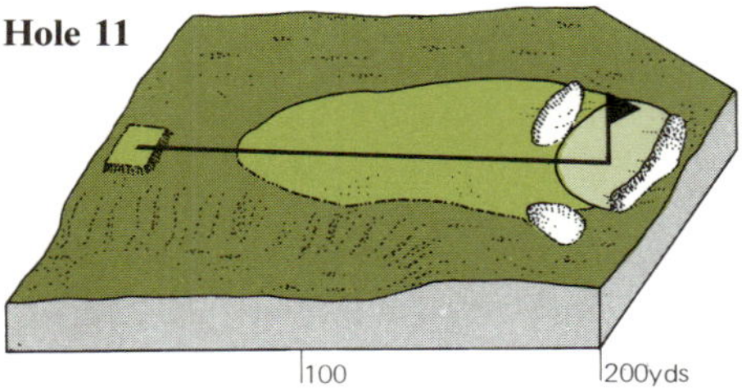


**Hole 12**

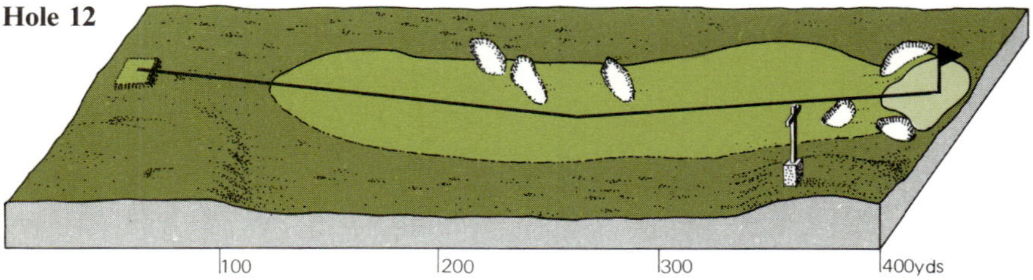

**Hole 13** 381 yards Par 4

One of the course's outstanding two-shot holes and known as 'Tickly Tap'.

Drive — From an elevated tee right on top of the hill, with a deceptive, 200-yard carry over a sandy waste, or a safer line to the right – avoiding the big bunker left, but leaving a more difficult 2nd.

2nd Shot — To a high, elevated, two-tier green, where three-putting is always a danger.

**Hole 14** 441 yards Par 4

'Risk-an-Hope' is a rather long two-shot, where you turn back towards the sea. The prevailing wind is from the left.

Drive — Fairly straightforward, but watch for the bunker jutting in from the left.

2nd Shot — Generally a wood or long iron to a tightly-bunkered green with a narrow entrance. The green slopes from the back and a putt from behind the hole can be tricky.

**Hole 15** 210 yards Par 3

A splendid short hole and, says Henry Longhurst, 'the most satisfying single stroke on the course if you happen to bring it off'. That can be difficult: you have to carry a wilderness of rough, bumps and hollows, with a deep pit front right of the green – a bunker waiting to catch you on its far side and three more on the left. 'Ca Canny' is the right name.

**Hole 16** 412 yards Par 4

'Wee Burn' crosses the fairway just in front of the green, in a similar way to Swilcan Burn on the first hole of the Old Course at St Andrews. It was the downfall of British hopes on the second day of the 1963 Walker Cup.

Drive — Governed by the bunker to the left, which pushes you over to the right.

2nd Shot — Not easy. You must carry both the burn and a high bank in front of the green, so something like a 5-iron is recommended.

**Hole 17** 498 yards Par 5

'Lang Whang' is the hole that ended Peter Oosterhuis's bid for victory in the 1972 John Player Classic, when he drove into the rough on the right and was still well short two shots later, enabling Bob Charles to go one up.

Drive — A blind tee shot, very long, with two traps on the right and high sandhills on the left.

2nd Shot — Over a big mound to the green, which may well be out of range if the wind is adverse. A big bunker short-right of the green is to be avoided and the long, narrow green has guardian bunkers on both sides.

**Hole 18** 431 yards Par 4

'Ailsa Hame'. Johnny Miller scored his last of three successive birdies here in the first round of the 1973 John Player Classic.

Drive — From an elevated tee, with a huge carry which is difficult for the average player. Two sand-traps jut into the fairway from the left and there are gorse bushes on the right, so it demands your straightest drive.

2nd Shot — If short, a gully in front of the green can kick your ball away left – and there are hillocks front left and right.

Hole 13

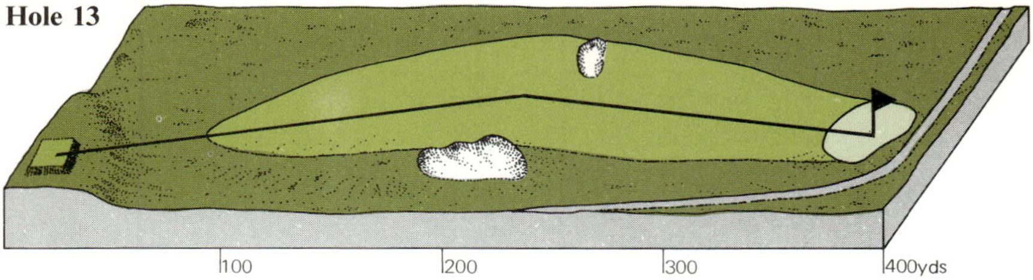


Hole 14

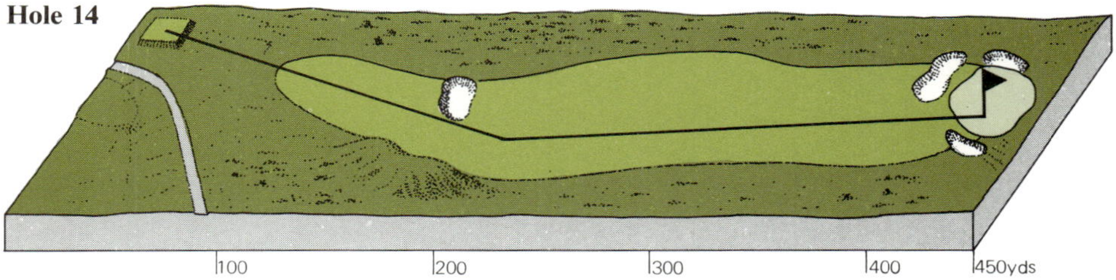


Hole 15

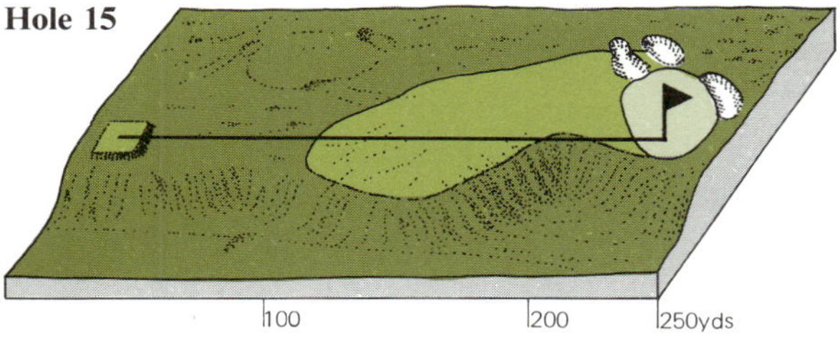


Hole 16

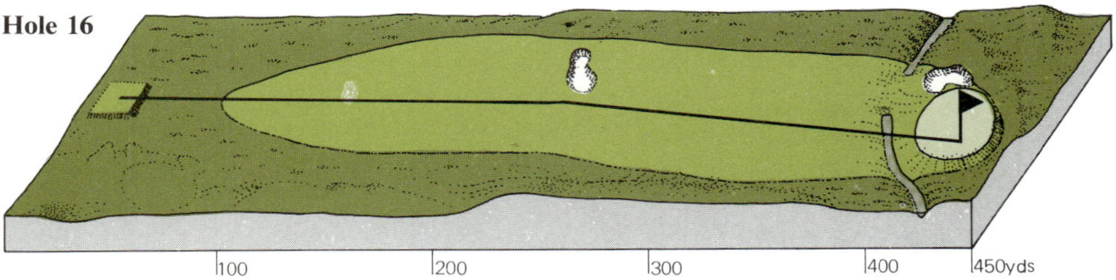


Hole 17

Hole 18

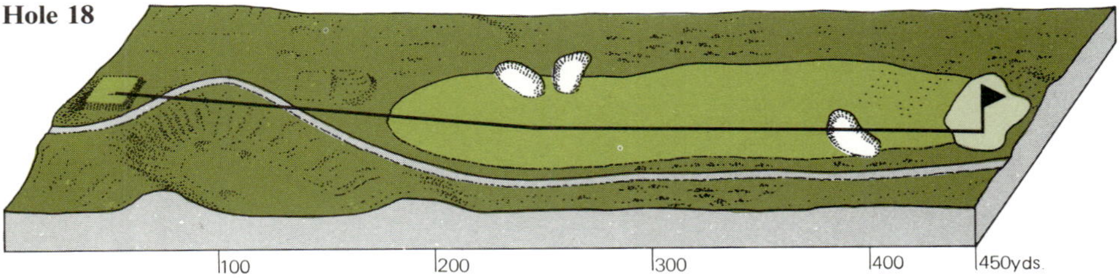

# Wentworth

## Piccadilly World Match Play Championship

Wentworth, where the Piccadilly World Match Play Championship has been held since its inception in 1964, has two championship courses and a nine-hole course, with a swimming pool, tennis courts and a ballroom among its country-club facilities. One of the few places of its kind in this country, it is a home-from-home for visiting American players. The club is cradled in Surrey woodland on the A30 road out of London, but the rumble of juggernaut lorries carrying freight to and from Southampton Docks is only a distant murmur to players on the East and West Courses.

It was the East Course which staged the first big international event at Wentworth, the Curtis Cup match of 1932, but it is the more difficult West Course, popularly known as the Burma Road, which has been the scene of the Ryder Cup, Canada (now World) Cup and, of course, the Piccadilly in more recent years.

Wentworth's West Course was also where the serious televising of golf by BBC began, with the 1953 Ryder Cup. 'It was before this Ryder Cup,' recalls commentator and writer Henry Longhurst, 'that Peter Roscow, so long Secretary of the Club, and held in such affectionate memory by all who knew him, received a letter from a lady asking for a ticket for her husband. He did not wish to play in the match, she said. He only wished to watch it.'

The Wentworth clubhouse, a fine period building, was once the home of Lady Anne Wellesley, sister of the famous Duke of Wellington, and during the Second World War it was to become the headquarters of the Chief of the Imperial General Staff, should London have been destroyed.

**Hole 1** 471 yards Par 4

The first hole has several times figured as the 19th in the World Match Play Championship and it can be a very testing start – or finish.

Drive: Over the approach road of the Clubhouse to a wide plateau fairway, which falls away into a valley and rises again to the green, with an awkward slope from right to left. A long tee shot down the left opens up the green, but the ball must be kept to the left of the fairway, as the ground slopes steeply to the right. Accuracy essential here – as it is with the second shot.

2nd Shot: Played over the valley, to carry the slope short of the green, which is trapped and surrounded by gorse bushes, trees and bunkers on both sides.

**Hole 2** 155 yards Par 3

Another valley hole, but a short one this time to a kidney-shaped plateau green, set in the rise on the other side. The front of the green is steeply banked with bunkers well placed under the drop at either side and a tree and bunker to the right. A small target and you need to be up.

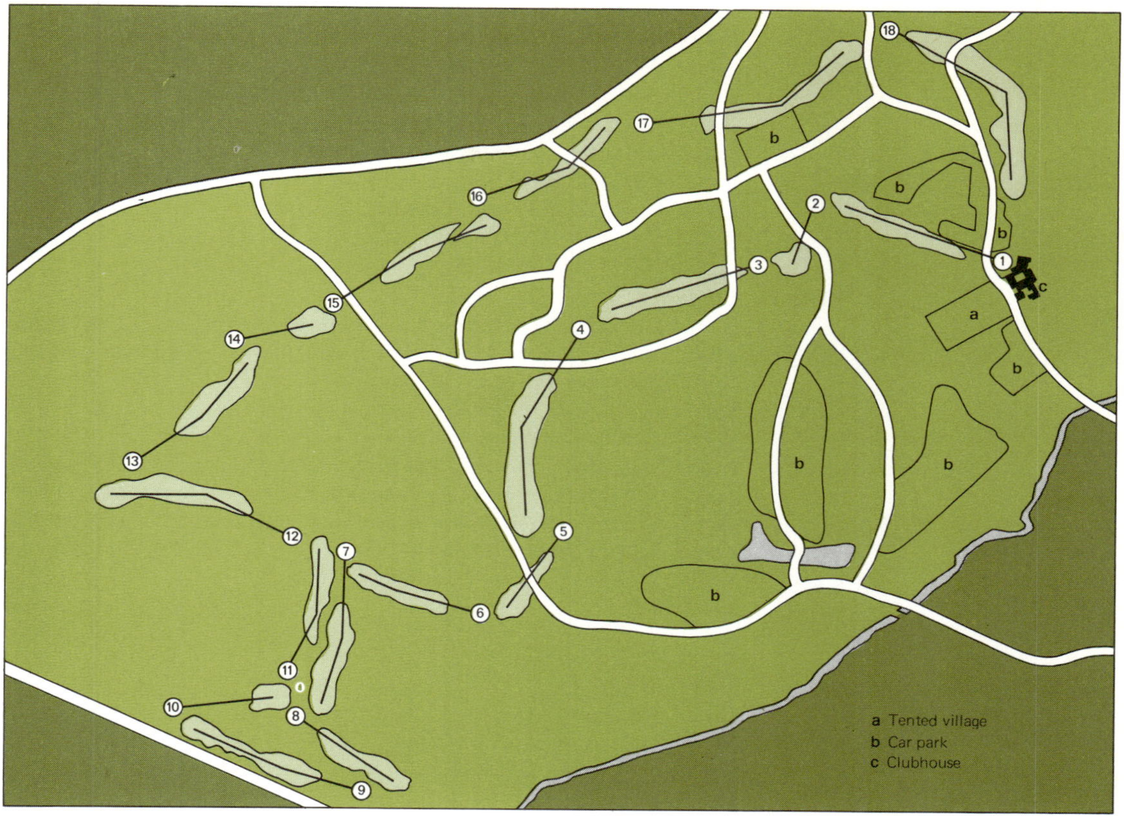


**Total length** 6969 yards
**Out** 3371 yards
**In** 3598 yards

**Hole 1**

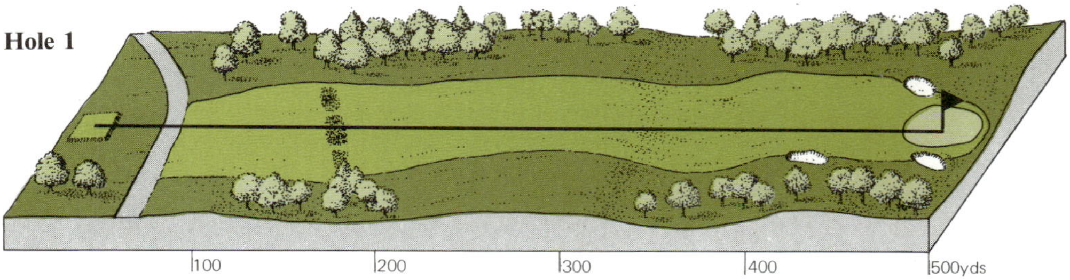


**Hole 2**

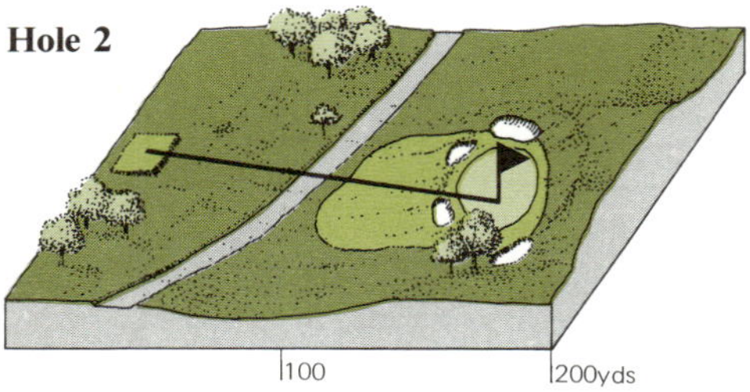

**Hole 3** 452 yards Par 4
A very long and difficult par 4, uphill, with trees forming a narrow tunnel right up to the two-tiered green, flanked on the left by rhododendron bushes.

Drive — Down the left-hand side, short of a bunker to the right at 250 yards.

2nd Shot — Uphill, must carry two bunkers, pitch short and be long enough to run up to the level of the two-tiered green. A full shot will not stay on the top level and this leaves a difficult one back, as the ground rises in the back of the green. And if you are short, it is easy to take three putts.

**Hole 4** 501 yards Par 5
A semi-dogleg to the left, with plenty of margin for error – a blind drive, out-of-bounds to the right and left, a brook, marshy ground and a large bunker protecting the green on the left.

Drive — Blind and downhill, with marker posts to give the correct line and a 50-yard carry over heather to put you in sight of the green.

2nd Shot — Has to be played *over* a ditch and marshy ground, with the green placed diagonally across the line of flight and the flag usually placed behind the guardian bunker. Played without draw and needs accurately judged length to avoid the bunker on back right.

**Hole 5** 191 yards Par 3
The second short hole in the first five, but it calls for great accuracy, as the narrow, oval green is surrounded by deep bunkers and is two-tiered. Only the top of the flag can be seen from the tee and the carry is over gorse and heather. A 4-iron is favoured, but Jacklin hit a 6-iron shot within a yard of the hole in the 1972 Piccadilly semi-final.

**Hole 6** 344 yards Par 4
One of the shorter par-4s, but the fairway slopes from right to left and can easily throw you into the rough. Heather along the right, woods on the left.

Drive — Should be played down the left side of the fairway over a large bunker, with a driver or long iron.

2nd Shot — A full pitch with 8- or 9-iron. The green is well guarded, with bunkers leading up to its front, two more under the drop on the left and a big one short on the right. A fast putting surface when you get there.

**Hole 7** 399 yards Par 4
Not an easy one. Arnold Palmer once drove into the trees on the left, then his second shot hit a tree in front of him and rebounded. The tee is set back in an alcove among the trees, facing a downhill slope to a shallow gulley fringed by gorse and bunkers on both sides.

Drive — Must be straight. Big hitters take an iron or lower wood, to avoid running into the heather at the bottom of the slope. Too far left and you are in the woods, too far right and you have an extremely difficult second shot, over trees and an enormous bunker on the front-right of the green.

2nd Shot — Up a steep rise over a stretch of wet, marshy ground to the double-tiered plateau green, with a very steep slope in the middle.

Hole 3

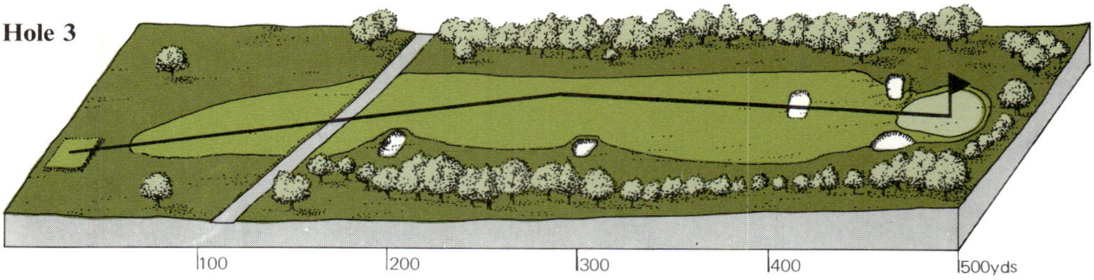


Hole 4

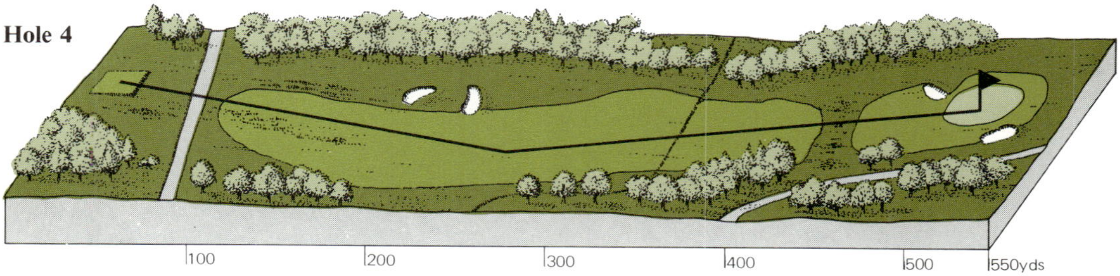


Hole 5

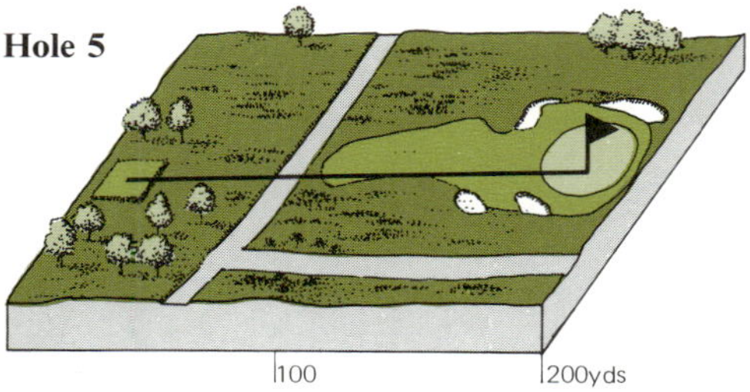


Hole 6

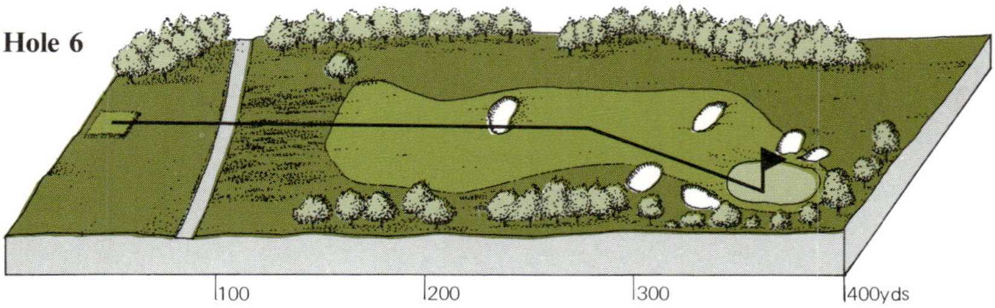


Hole 7

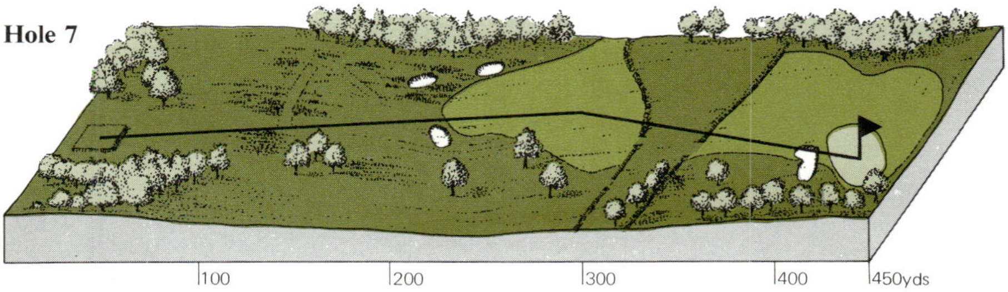

**Hole 8** 398 yards Par 4

Full of character, with a wide fairway to drive into, and a ditch running across diagonally. Then there is a wide pond and, while this is no problem to the professional, it can be a great hazard to the club player.

Drive A driver is often unwise here for the downhill shot to the right side of a narrow fairway almost surrounded by heather and trees and sloping into deep rough on the left.

2nd Shot Over the pond to a built-up green, which can be reached from the neck of the fairway with a medium iron. Beware the green's drop away to woods on the left.

**Hole 9** 460 yards Par 4

Scene of the famous 1966 confrontation between Jack Nicklaus and Col. A. A. Duncan, the referee (see p. 31). There is an uphill slope to a wide fairway, with a long carry of heather and bracken for the average player. And there is heather again down on the right for the fading drive.

Drive Long and down the middle, with the slope of the fairway taking it right.

2nd Shot A wood, over the narrow pass formed by converging cross bunkers a hundred yards from the green, which is guarded by a particularly good bunker on the left and trees on the right, awaiting the off-line shot.

**Hole 10** 186 yards Par 3

One of the finest short holes in Britain. There is heather all the way to the green, the middle right half of which is covered by a tall clump of trees. The green itself is flat and elevated, built out of the shoulder of a left-hand ridge, with a sharp drop away on the right. A high stopping shot, with a little draw, will often run up the bank and back into the hole area.

**Hole 11** 376 yards Par 4

During the 1956 Canada Cup, Ben Hogan stood seven-under-fours on the 11th tee. His drive found a bad lie on the edge of the wood on the left, he took three more to reach the green and finally holed out in six. The hole is a semi-dogleg to the left. The tee is high, with a long carry over heather and two ditches.

Drive Should land in the valley in the centre of the fairway, beyond the bunker on the right.

2nd Shot Must be bold, to carry the large cross-bunkers at the front of the green, which slopes from back to front.

**Hole 12** 483 yards Par 5

This was a critical hole for Arnold Palmer, in his semi-final with Gary Player in the 1966 World Match Play. He was over the back of the green in two, then left his approach woefully short and three-putted. Player got a birdie, putting Palmer three down and he lost 3 & 2. The character of the hole is provided by the tall fir trees that cross the fairway 180 yards from the tee.

Drive Must carry the line of trees and be as far down the right as possible, otherwise the second shot is blind.

2nd Shot Trees all along the left-hand side and a big bunker on the front right of the green. Over the green is out of bounds.

**Hole 8**

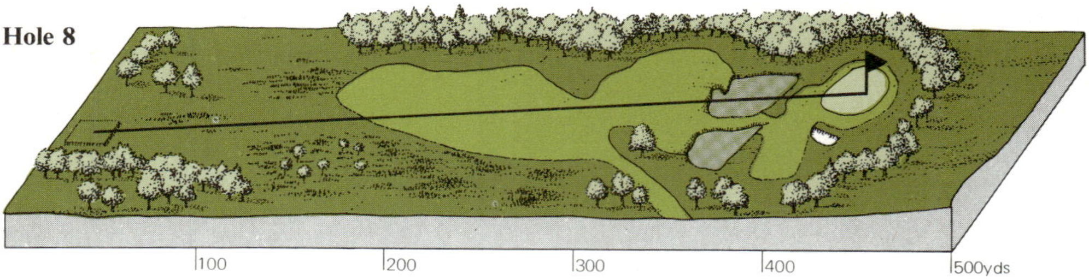


**Hole 9**

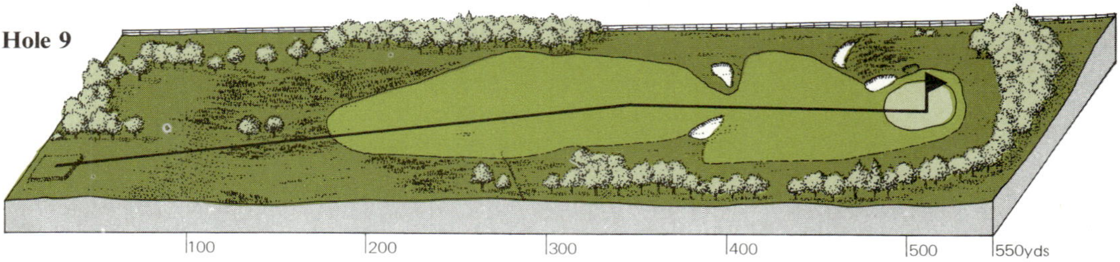


**Hole 10**

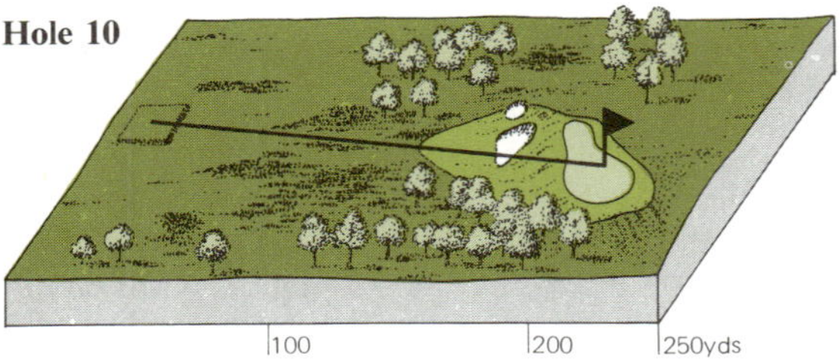


**Hole 11**

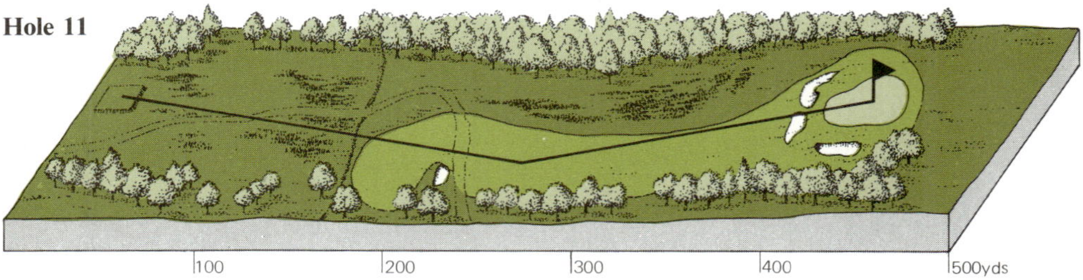


**Hole 12**

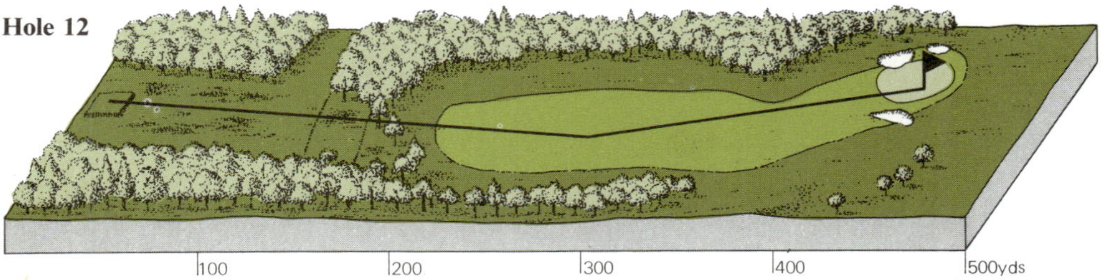

**Hole 13** 441 yards Par 4

Trouble all the way on the left, so you should go out to the right, then turn half-left and over the deep ditch across the fairway and up to the green.

Drive — Uphill down the right and must be long to provide a view of the green with the 2nd shot.

2nd Shot — Trees at the end of the ditch mask the flag, but the green will gather the ball.

**Hole 14** 179 yards Par 3

Last of the course's short holes. Uphill all the way to a double-tiered green, bounded by bunkers on the left. Trees protect the right side all the way from tee to green and beyond; the prevailing wind usually against you. Plenty of club needed. Watch the double terracing on the green: pitches to the top layer have a nasty habit of rolling down again.

**Hole 15** 480 yards Par 5

As with almost every hole at Wentworth, you drive down an avenue of trees to a narrow fairway.

Drive — Down the left to carry sixty yards of rough and the bunker on the left. Too far right and the second shot will catch the bunker on the right, or roll down left into the bunker on that side.

2nd Shot — A long one over a ditch to the green, which slopes from right to left and is well guarded.

**Hole 16** 380 yards Par 4

Far more difficult than it looks, this short dogleg, with trees on either side of the fairway, though the bunkers on the left will worry only handicap players.

Drive — From a tee set close to the wood, which curves to the right.

2nd Shot — Usually no more than an 8-iron and must carry the bunker just short of and to the right of the green, which has a bank at the back.

**Hole 17** 571 yards Par 5

Longest hole on the course and a tremendous par 5. Bruce Devlin put his 2nd shot out of bounds here in the 1964 Piccadilly semi-final and it cost him the match. Arnold Palmer was out of bounds in the 1966 Piccadilly.

Drive — Downhill, with an out-of-bounds fence on the left, trees and rough on the right, where a large fir is particularly menacing.

2nd Shot — Unlikely to reach the green, unless a bold shot is attempted. Played through a bottleneck of trees from the abrupt dogleg. The ground to the right of the green falls sharply away into the woods.

**Hole 18** 502 yards Par 5

Another dogleg, this time to the right, with considerable distance to the bend.

Drive — Must be a good one to the centre of the fairway, if the green is to be opened for the second shot.

2nd Shot — A long iron or wood, over a dip and ditch to a green guarded by a semicircle of trees, with the bunker on the left claiming shots that are not hit for the back of the green.

**Hole 13**

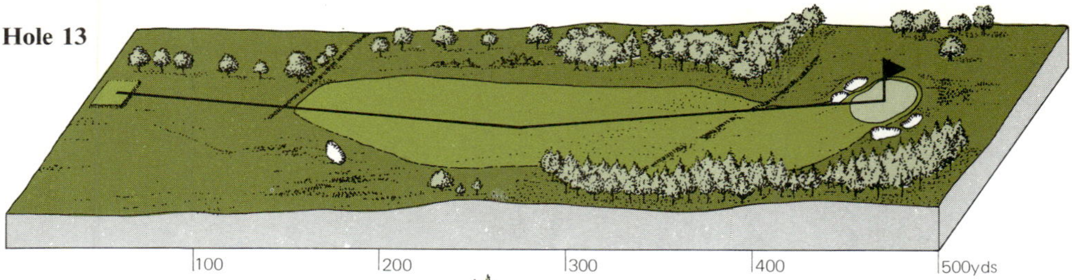


**Hole 14**

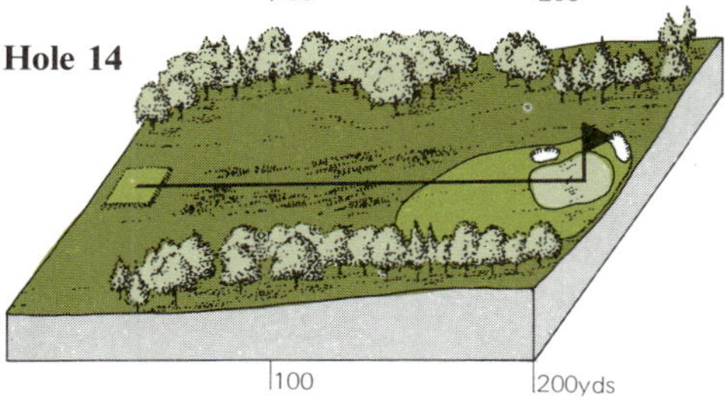


**Hole 15**

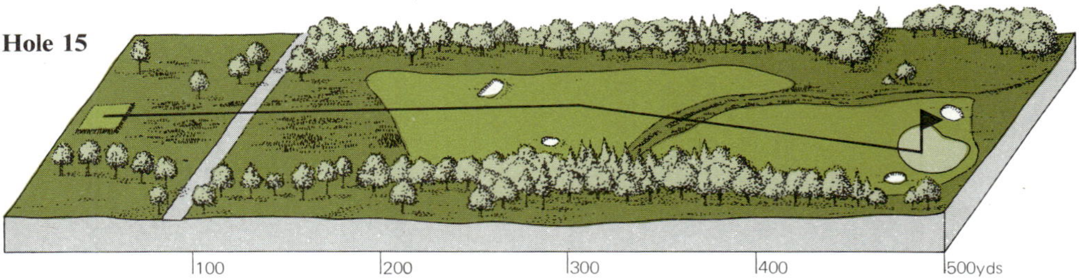


**Hole 16**

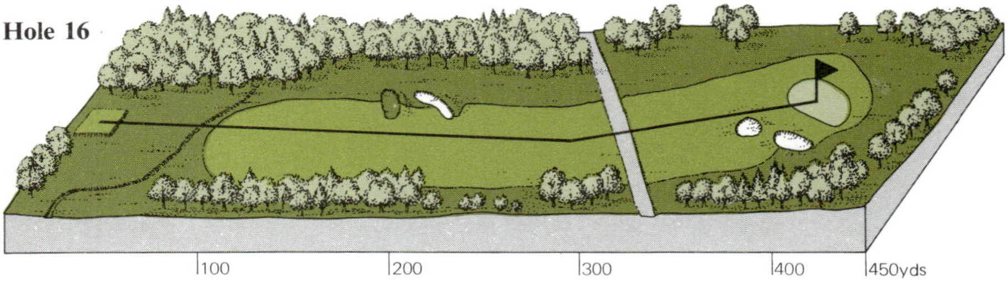


**Hole 17**

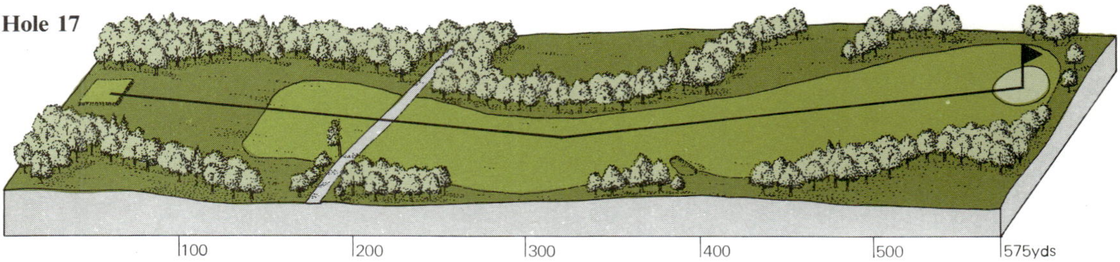


**Hole 18**

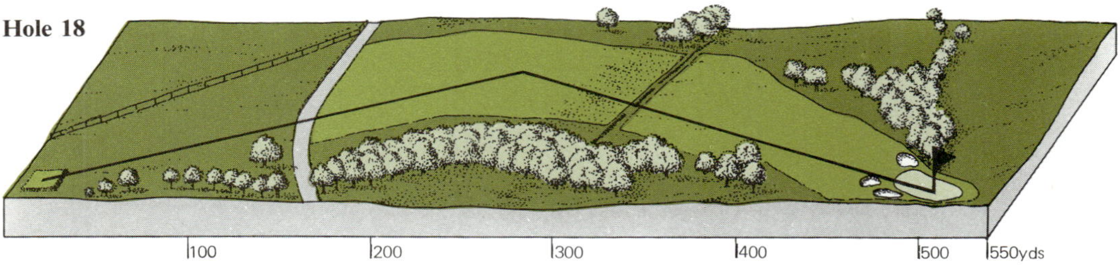

Lee Trevino

# 4 The players

## A hundred of the best

**Tommy Aaron**
Born 22.2.37, Gainesville, Georgia, USA. Turned pro 1960, after playing in Walker Cup, but had to wait nine years for first big win, the 1969 Canadian Open, after earning 'always-the-bridesmaid' tag by finishing second in nine events on US Tour. Won US Masters 1973. US Ryder Cup team 1969–73. Best Tour year 1972, $118,924 (9th).

Tall, smooth, elegant swinger. When he takes the club back from the ball, it goes sharply in round the back of his right foot, making it look as if he is going to swing well inside the backswing. In fact, he doesn't: the swing is up and down, rather wristy-looking, but very smooth. An excellent putter, but here again keeps the putter blade shut as it goes away from the ball in the backswing.

**Brian ('Buddy') Allin**
Born 13.10.44, Bremerton, Wash., USA. Like Johnny Miller, was a member of the Mormon Brigham Young University golf team, but otherwise had an undistinguished amateur career. Turned pro 1970, after Army service in Vietnam, and won the Greater Greensboro Open in the same year. His second Tour win was in 1973, when he was 33rd in the US money list with $77,472; he finished 23-under par in the Florida Citrus Open, eight strokes in front of the field – two records for the year's American circuit. Allin confirmed his 'arrival' with two more Tour wins in 1974, finishing ninth in the money list with $137,950.

**Peter Alliss**
Born 28.2.31, Berlin. Turned pro 1946, when 15. Represented Britain in Ryder Cup 1953–57–59–61–63–65–67–69 and England in World (formerly Canada) Cup 1954–55–57–58–59–61–62–66–67. Won PGA Championship 1957–62–65. Captained England in 1967 Home Internationals.

Strongly built and with his feet planted firmly on the ground, Alliss is one of the game's big hitters. On his own admission, however, his short game and putting have not always reached the same high standard. Although still competing at top level, he has built a reputation as one of the game's best-informed commentators in recent years.

**George Archer** *(left)*
Born 1.10.39, Gilroy, Calif., USA. Started as caddie when 12 and has been playing ever since. Turned pro 1964. Won his first of eleven US Tour events in 1965, the PGA Team Championship (with Bobby Nichols) in 1968 and US Masters 1969. Best Tour year 1968, $150,972 (4th).

At 6ft 6in. is one of the tallest men on US circuit and has a willowy swing, but is among world's greatest putters. Keeps his feet together and the ball right off the edge of his left toe. When on form, makes putting look all too simple.

**Hugh Baiocchi** *(below)*
Born 17.8.46, South Africa. Won South African Amateur title 1970 and turned pro following year. Has won several important tournaments in his own country and 1973 Swiss Open. Runner-up (with Gary Player) World Cup team event 1973.

**Harry Bannerman** *(above)*
Born 5.3.42, Aberdeen. Scottish boy international 1959. Turned pro 1965, after winning Scottish Alliance title. Scottish pro champion 1967–72, British Ryder Cup team 1971 and represented Scotland in World Cup 1967–72.

Has wide, wristy swing and is a positive putter. Note his fairly wide stance on the greens, how he keeps his left wrist firm when putting and gives the ball a nice, firm hit, after lining it up with the crease of his left trouser leg.

**Miller Barber**
Born 31.3.31, Shreveport, Louisiana, USA. Turned pro 1958 and won his first Tour event six years later, winning another eight since, including 1973 World Open championship, with record £40,000 prize. US Ryder Cup team 1969–71. Known for years as 'Mr X' by fellow pros, because of his aloofness. Best Tour year 1973, $184,014 (6th).

Has strange, seemingly five-piece backswing, everything appearing to go in different directions, with the clubface very closed at the top, but when he reaches the hitting area the blade is dead on, pointing straight at the target. An excellent putter.

**Brian Barnes**

Born 3.6.45, Addington, Surrey. British Youths Champion 1964, then turned pro. Protégé of his father-in-law, Max Faulkner. Won Australian Masters 1970, Dutch Open 1974. British Ryder Cup team 1969–71–73, Scottish World Cup team 1974.

A giant of a man. Seems to hold his head rather to left at address position, as if looking at ball with only his left eye. Slow, deliberate backswing, but gives the ball the most tremendous thrash. Has the excellent putting touch which seems to be speciality of most big pros.

**Frank Beard**

Born 1.5.39, Dallas, Texas, USA. Turned pro 1962 and won first Tour event in following year, collecting another ten since – his last the 1971 Greater New Orleans Open. US Ryder Cup team 1969–71. Top US Tour money-winner 1969, with $175,224.

Very good swing and excellent short game. One of the new breed of professionals, who looks on golf and golf courses rather like a lawyer looks at going to the office.

**Maurice Bembridge**

Born 21.2.45, Worksop, Notts. Turned pro 1960. Main wins include 1969 News of the World PGA Match Play, 1971 Dunlop Masters, 1974 Piccadilly Medal, Double Diamond and Viyella PGA. Regularly winters abroad, covering South Africa, Australia, New Zealand and Far East, and has won money in all five continents. British Ryder Cup team 1969–71–73, English World Cup team 1974.

Very compact player, with solid, three-quarter backswing and good, firm grip. His legs come into the ball and he hits it down and through with very firm wrists.

**Roberto Bernardini**

Born 21.1.44, Rome, Italy. Turned pro 1966. Wins include Swiss Open 1968–69, Italian Native Open 1967–68 and Lancia d'Oro Open three times. Has represented Italy eight times in World Cup, played once in US Masters and several times in British Open.

**Homero Blancas**
Born 7.3.38, Houston, Texas, USA. Caused sensation by shooting 55 on par-70 course at Longview, Texas, in 1961. Turned pro 1963. Won Mexican Open 1965, when he was named Rookie of the year, and has since collected another four Tour events. US Ryder Cup team 1973. Best Tour year 1970, $100,994 (16th).

**Julius Boros**
Born 3.3.20, Fairfield, Connecticut, USA. Turned pro 1949 and has twice been top money-winner on Tour (1952–55). Won US Open 1952–63, US PGA 1968 and old 'World' Championship 1952–55. Finished 2nd (with Lee Trevino) 1968 World Cup. US Player of the Year 1952–63. US Ryder Cup team 1959–63–65–67. Family man with six children. Best Tour year 1968, $148,310 (5th).

Reminiscent of the great Alfred Padgham, a British star of the 30s. Gives the impression, as he stands to the ball, that everything is fine and relaxed; the grip doesn't look too tense, the swing is easy and smooth. Everything from his drive to the putt is the most relaxed thing you have ever seen on a golf course.

**Gay Brewer** *(left)*
Born 19.3.32, Middletown, Ohio, USA. Turned pro 1956 and has won 11 events on Tour, including 1967 US Masters and 1972 Canadian Open. US Ryder Cup team 1967–73. Best Tour year 1973, $93,502.

Quick player, with slight loop in backswing. Hits the ball very hard. One of the world's great putters when his game is on.

**Peter Butler** *(below)*
Born 25.3.32, Birmingham. Turned pro 1949. Wins include 1968 French Open, 1971 Grand Bahama Open, 1974 Sumrie-Bournemouth (with Clive Clark). British Ryder Cup team 1965–69–71–73. England World Cup team 1969–70–73. Played in US Masters 1964–66.

**Billy Casper**

Born 24.6.31, San Diego, Calif., USA. Turned pro 1954, winning first Tour event in 1956 and his 50th, the Greater Hartford Open, in 1973. Wins include US Open 1959–66, Masters 1970, Canadian Open 1967. Passed $1 million in prize money 1970. US Player of the Year 1966–70. US Ryder Cup team 1961–63–65–67–69–71–73. Top US money-winner 1966 and 1968 ($205,168). Won Lancome Trophy 1974. Mormon convert in 1966, gives his church 10 per cent of winnings and lists his interests as religion, family, golf and fishing 'in that order'. Has many allergies and cannot play Florida courses because of turf dressing used in that State.

One of the most refreshing players to watch, makes it look as though he is just out for an afternoon round. Strides along, takes club out of bag, sometimes wipes blade on left sock, then up to the ball, one quick look and it's on its way. Still has reputation of being world's best putter, but may have been overtaken by some of younger generation in this respect. Overall brilliance of his game, rather than brilliant putting, has kept him at the top.

**Bob Charles**

Born 14.3.36, Christchurch, New Zealand. Turned pro 1960 and won 1963 British Open, after tie with Phil Rodgers, becoming first left-hander and New Zealander to do so. Joint 2nd 1968 British Open and second again in following year. World Cup team runner-up (with W. Godfrey) 1967. Won Piccadilly World Match Play 1969, John Player Classic 1972, New Zealand and South African Opens 1973, Swiss Open 1974. Five wins on US Tour include 1968 Canadian Open and 1974 Greater Greensboro Open. Best US Tour 1967, $72,468 (11th).

Uses short, three-quarter backswing, with long follow through. Firm, slow backswing, but good acceleration through the ball. Wonderful putter, with good, easy stance, crouching over from the waist, but putter and arm seem to work as unit, taken slowly back from ball and through, with head still.

**Clive Clark** *(below)*
Born 27.6.45, Winchester, Hants. Runner-up British Amateur 1965. Walker Cup team 1965, Britain *v.* Continent of Europe 1964–65. Turned pro 1965. Won Danish Open 1966, Sumrie-Bournemouth (with Peter Butler) 1974. Leading British player 1967 British Open (joint 3rd). British Ryder Cup team 1973.

**Jim Colbert** *(above)*
Born 9.3.41, Elizabeth, NJ, USA. Went to Kansas State University on an American football scholarship, but lost his taste for the game when having several front teeth knocked out in a freshmen's match. Switched to golf, turning pro in 1965. Has won four US Tour events, including the American Classic in 1974, his most successful year with $96,734 winnings and 21st place on the money list.

**Bobby Cole** *(above)*
Born 11.5.48, Springs, South Africa. Won British Amateur 1966, when 18. Turned pro 1967. Won South African Dunlop Masters 1969, World Cup individual and team (with Dale Hayes) and South African Open 1974. Best US Tour year 1974, $59,616.

Attributes long hitting to wide arc in his swing, extensive use of legs and timing his clubhead speed at the bottom. Has modelled many of his shots on Gary Player, particularly with wedge, where his knees are kept close together, arms high, hands well forward, shortish backswing and takes a big divot as he goes down and through the ball.

**Neil Coles** *(left)*
Born 26.9.34, London. Consistent player, but makes few appearances overseas, because he dislikes air travel. Regular member Britain's Ryder Cup team since 1961. Won Spanish Open and Benson & Hedges 1973, Wills Open 1974. Joint second British Open 1973.

Strong left-hand grip, showing practically all the knuckles on left hand. Turns clubface in at address position and gets ball well back near the heel of the club. A rather round, yet simple swing, doesn't waste time and is fine putter.

**Charles Coody**
Born 13.7.37, Stamford, Texas, USA. Turned pro 1963 and has won three Tour events, including 1971 Masters, also 1971 World Series and 1973 John Player Classic. US Ryder Cup team 1971. Best Tour year 1971, $94,947.

Tall, slim man who, from the hitting area through the ball, seems to drop his right shoulder down and across the flight. When putting, pulls his left trouser up a little at knee, and loosens clothing before almost every swing.

**Bruce Crampton**
Born 28.9.35, Sydney, Australia. Turned pro 1953 and has won 14 events on US Tour, including four in 1973. Won 1956 Australian Open when 20. Regular on US Tour since 1957 and was second highest money-winner 1973, with $274,266. Australia's World Cup team 1972. Despite not winning in America during 1974, he still finished 12th on the money list with $131,356.

One of the longest hitters in world golf, but has had little success in Britain. Very good short game, allied to strong hitting. Slow backswing and generates great power with wide swing.

**Ben Crenshaw**
Born 11.1.52, Austin, Texas, USA. While at University of Texas won National Collegiate championship three times, sharing it with Tom Kite in 1972, tieing for third place in the Heritage Classic in the same year, when still an amateur, and was a member of the US World Amateur Cup team. Turned pro 1973, earning $76,749 from nine Tour events played as a professional and winning the San Antonio–Texas Open. Also finished joint second to Miller Barber in the World Open, earning Barber's comment that: 'Today I felt as if I beat the coming star. I strongly believe this.' His view of 'Gentle Ben' is shared by many critics.

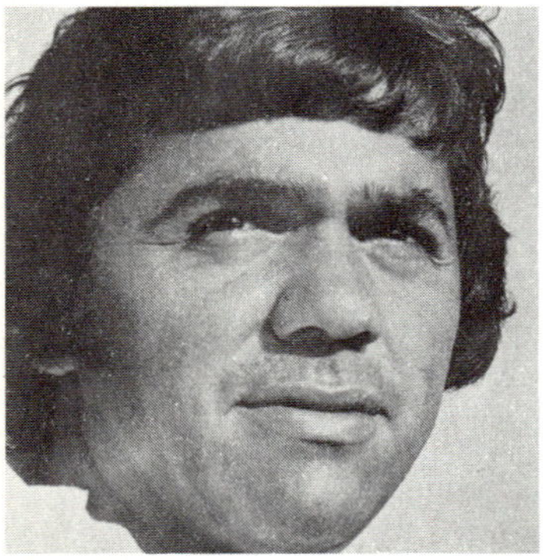

**Rod Curl**
Born 9.1.43, Redding, Calif., USA. A three-quarter Wintu Indian, did not take up golf until he was 19, having concentrated on baseball at high school. Turned pro 1968 and says his early years on US Tour were mainly spent learning what most other players already knew. Made his breakthrough in 1974 by winning Colonial Open and finishing 17th on money list with $120,154.

**Craig DeFoy**

Born 27.3.47, Pennsylvania, USA. Welsh father and is naturalised Briton. Turned pro 1963. Finished 4th in 1971 British Open, three strokes down on Trevino. Won Zambian Open 1972–73. Welsh World Cup team 1971–73–74.

Tall, slim, rather deliberate player. One would like to see him attacking the ball more.

**Roberto de Vicenzo**

Born 14.4.23, Buenos Aires, Argentina. Turned pro 1938 and won Argentine Open for first of eight times in 1944. First competed in British Open 1948 and won it, aged 44, in 1967. Won World Cup individual 1962, team (with A. Cerda) 1953 and team runner-up four times. Joined US Tour 1947 and has won nine events. Tied for play-off with Bob Goalby in 1968 US Masters on his 45th birthday, but lost a stroke and possible victory when his playing card was found to have been wrongly marked by playing partner, Tommy Aaron. Won Brazilian Open for sixth time 1973, Pringle World 1974. Best Tour year 1967, $42,091.

One of the greatest-ever strikers of the ball. Gives himself plenty of room to swing, standing well away from the ball and reaching out to it with his arms. A big man, with tremendous shoulder turn. Delicate player round the green, with little chips and bunker shots, though putting has troubled him in recent years.

**Bruce Devlin**

Born 10.10.37, Armidale, Australia. Now lives in Florida. Won 1959 Australian Amateur, and, still an amateur, the 1960 Australian Open. Turned pro 1961 and joined US Tour in following year. Nine Tour victories include Alcan and two other events in 1970, when he also teamed with David Graham to win World Cup. Best Tour year 1972, $119,768 (8th).

Very short backswing, not much longer than Doug Sanders. Simple-looking movement, though sometimes tends to get a little shut, causing problems, but often gets away with this by long, flowing follow through. Very good short game.

**Gardner Dickinson**

Born 27.9.27, Dothan, Alabama, USA. Turned pro 1952 and won first of eight Tour events in 1956. US Ryder Cup team 1967–71. Best Tour year 1968, $73,354.

Small in stature, but a great course tactician, with complete concentration. An excellent teacher, whom many professionals consult, as he probably knows more about the workings of a golf swing than anyone in the world.

**Lee Elder**

Born 14.7.34, Dallas, Texas, USA. Turned pro 1959 and first attracted attention with play-off against Nicklaus for 1968 American Golf Classic, losing after five holes. First Tour win the 1974 Monsanto Open. Won Nigerian Open 1971, playing in South Africa – at Gary Player's invitation – during the same trip, despite that country's apartheid policy towards coloured sportsmen. Best US Tour year 1973, $84,730 (30th).

A player of even temperament, once said he could not afford the risk of banging clubs on the ground in case he broke them.

**Forrest Fezler**

Born 23.9.49, Hayward, Calif., USA. Won California State Amateur title 1969, after losing to Johnny Miller in previous year's semi-finals. Turned pro 1969 and joined Tour via 1971 qualifying school. Dubbed 'Fuzzy' because of his hair-style and moustache, he finished 13th on 1973 money list with $106,390, after being runner-up in three events, including Canadian Open. Won his first Tour event, Southern Open, in 1974, was second to Hale Irwin in US Open, picked up another $90,066, and this quiet young man is clearly one to be watched closely.

**Ray Floyd**

Born 4.9.42, Fort Bragg, N. Carolina, USA. Seriously considered baseball as a playing career, but opted for golf after winning International Junior Chamber of Commerce title in 1960 and turned pro in 1961. Won first Tour event in 1963 and four since, including 1969 US PGA. US Ryder Cup team 1969. Best Tour year 1974, $119,385 (18th).

Slight wristiness by American standards may account for some inconsistency over the years. Very closed clubface at top of backswing. Hits ball squarely and for great distances when in form.

**Rod Funseth**

Born 3.4.33, Spokane, Wash., USA. Turned pro 1956, joined US Tour five years later and has regularly been in the top 100 money-winners since finishing 101st in 1962. His first win on the circuit came in 1965, but he had to wait until January 1973 for his second, when collecting the first event, the Glen Campbell Los Angeles Open in his best month of golf, about which he commented: 'I'm not putting that well, but the ball keeps going in the hole.' Best Tour year 1973, $89,145 (29th).

**Bernard Gallacher** *(below)*

Born 9.2.49, Bathgate, Scotland. Turned pro 1967. Became youngest-ever member of British Ryder Cup team in 1969 and retained his place in 1971–3. Won Carrolls International, Dunlop Masters 1974. Scottish Professional Champion 1971–3. Scottish World Cup team 1969–71–74.

A slight figure, but hits ball very hard. Fine touch round the greens and, since sorting out his driving, should go on from strength to strength.

**Jean Garaialde** *(above)*

Born 2.10.34, Ciboure, France. Turned pro 1952. Has won Open championships of France, Germany, Morocco, Spain and Sweden and many times winner of both French Native and PGA titles. Has represented France 17 times in World Cup.

Has slow, deliberate backswing and stands close in to ball, with upright stance.

**John Garner** *(left)*

Born 9.1.47, Preston, Lancs. Turned pro 1963. A controversial selection for Britain's 1971 Ryder Cup team, he subsequently won the Coca-Cola Young Pros title in a successful year. Selected for 1973 Ryder Cup team, but did not play. Won Benson & Hedges PGA Match Play 1972.

**Al Geiberger**
Born 1.9.37, Red Bluff, Calif., USA. Turned pro 1959, joining US Tour in following year. Won four Tour events before landing 1966 US PGA. Despite picking up prize money in 24 tournaments in 1967, he was not able to win another Tour event until the Sahara Invitational of 1974, a year in which he showed a welcome return to form and won $91,628.

**Bob Goalby**
Born 14.3.31, Belleville, Illinois, USA. Turned pro and joined US Tour 1957, winning first of 11 events on it – including the 1968 Masters – in the following year. US Ryder Cup team 1963. Best Tour year 1967, $77,107 (10th).

Strong player, who hits low-flying shots with every club. Improved his driving in 1970 by adding an inch to the shafts of his woods and irons, because he had found himself squatting too much when addressing the ball.

**David Graham** *(below)*
Born 23.5.46, Windsor, Australia. Now lives in Florida. Started work as an apprentice pro at 14, became a full pro at 18 and was declared bankrupt three years later, with business debts of £3,000, which subsequently he paid off from tournament winnings. Won World Cup team event (with Bruce Devlin) 1970. Joined US Tour 1971 and has won one event, with highest winnings $61,625 in 1974.

This great prospect hits the ball very low, giving himself a big advantage in bad weather.

**Lou Graham** *(above)*
Born 7.1.38, Nashville, Tennessee, USA. Turned pro 1962 after 30 months in US Army. Joined Tour 1964 and has won two events and been a consistent money-winner. Finished 19th in 1972 Tour money list with $96,077 and 19th again in 1973 with $94,854. US Ryder Cup team 1973.

**Hubert Green**

Born 28.12.46, Birmingham, Alabama, USA. Graduated from Florida State University 1968 and had to turn down selection for US Walker Cup team in that year, because of his prior decision to turn pro, a step he took in 1970. Won his first Tour event in 1971, two more in 1973 and four in 1974, finishing 3rd in the money list with $211,709. Lists his hobbies as 'bridge, hunting and other sports, antique collecting, nature and chess'.

From a distance seems to 'flap' at the ball with a very short backswing and says, 'I work on driving the clubhead through with a strong hip and knee action.' Improved his putting greatly in 1973 by using more upright stance.

**Malcolm Gregson** *(left)*

Born 15.8.43, Leicester. Turned pro 1961. Most successful year 1967, with tournament wins in the Schweppes PGA, Daks and Martini International, Ryder and World Cup selection, the Vardon Trophy as No. 1 in Britain's Order of Merit and £8,250 in prize money.

Easy backswing, excellent chipper of the ball and good putter. Learned his putting grip from one of the great Japanese artists and it all seems to fit into place like a jigsaw puzzle, with his fingers welded into one unit.

**Dale Hayes** *(above)*

Born 1.7.52, Zwartkop Country Club, South Africa, where his father is pro. As amateur won World Junior 1969, South African Stroke Play 1969–70, Scottish Amateur 1970, German Amateur 1970. Turned pro 1970 and won Spanish Open in following year, when 18. Won World Cup team (with Bobby Cole), S. African PGA and Coca-Cola Young Pros in 1974.

Tall and strong, hits ball with great power and a good touch. Could take over from Gary Player as South Africa's leading golfer.

**Jerry Heard**

Born 1.5.47, Visalia, Calif., USA. Turned pro 1968 and joined US Tour in following year, winning first big event, the American Golf Classic, in 1971. Won Florida Citrus and Spanish Opens 1974. Best Tour year 1974, $145,788 (8th).

Attributes success from 1970 onwards to the stability and changed mental outlook he developed after marrying in May of that year.

**Harold Henning**

Born 3.10.34, Johannesburg, S. Africa. One of three brothers, all golfers. Turned pro 1953. Won World Cup team event (with Gary Player) 1965 and was second in 1966–71. Also represented South Africa 1957–58–59–61–67–70. Has won two US Tour events, including 1970 Tallahassee Open, where he had a birdie, eagle, birdie on the last three holes. National title-winner in South Africa, Denmark, Germany, Italy, Switzerland, Malaya. Best money-winning year 1967, $80,000.

One of golf's fastest players, with quick, decisive actions: up to the ball, one, two, three, bang, it's on its way. Previously a magnificent putter, but lost touch when changing to cross-handed style for a time.

**Dave Hill**

Born 20.5.37, Jackson, Michigan, USA. Turned pro 1958 and scored first of his eleven Tour wins – including four Memphis Opens – in 1961. US Ryder Cup team 1969–73. Won Houston Open 1974. Best Tour year 1969, $156,423 (2nd).

A nervous player, loses up to two stone in weight during season. Obsessed with technical perfection, says: 'I want to get to the point where I master the golf ball the way Ben Hogan mastered it.'

**Mike Hill**

Born 27.1.39, Jackson, Michigan, USA. Turned pro 1967 and was often mistaken for elder brother, Dave, until establishing his own identity by winning 1970 Doral–Eastern Open. Best Tour year 1974, $76,802.

Less technically minded and more cautious than Dave, always plays first two rounds to survive 36-hole cut.

**Larry Hinson**

Born 5.8.44, Gastonia, N. Carolina, USA. Natural left-hander, recovered from polio attack at age of five that paralysed and withered his left arm. First played golf when 15. Turned pro 1968 and won 1969 New Orleans Open a year after graduating from qualifying school. Best Tour year 1970, $120,897 (8th).

Says his withered left arm has been a golfing advantage, because it was subsequently wrongly set when he broke it and 'now I can't turn it over, consequently there is no way I can duck-hook the ball'. His big swing almost knocks him off balance when he uses a wood and often produces a vicious hook, however.

**Tommy Horton** *(left)*

Born 16.6.41, St Helens, Lancs. Started playing golf at Royal Jersey club when five years old and captained their juniors when 11. Left school and turned pro 1957. Joined PGA circuit 1964. Won South African Open 1970, a year in which his world winnings were £9,500, and Penfold 1974. Unbeaten in 1971 home internationals.

Uses his hands well, whips through the ball very quickly and, for someone of his height and build, hits the ball a long way. Has been coached by Max Faulkner and picked up several of his mannerisms, particularly on the greens.

**Brian Huggett** *(above)*

Born 18.11.36, Porthcawl, Wales. Turned pro 1951. Won British Dunlop Masters 1970, Portuguese Open 1974. Joint runner-up British Open 1965, third 1962. Awarded Vardon Trophy 1968. British Ryder Cup team 1963–67–69–71–73. Welsh World Cup team 1963–64–65–66–68–69–70–71.

Player of great concentration: gets settled, a few waggles, slow, deliberate backswing, hits down through – and never gives up.

**Bernard Hunt**

Born 2.2.30, Atherstone, Warwicks. Turned pro on leaving school 1946. Won Egyptian Open 1956, Belgian Open 1957, German Open 1961, Brazilian Open 1962, French Open 1967, Algarve Open 1969, British Dunlop Masters 1963–65. Awarded Vardon Trophy 1958–60–61. British Ryder Cup team 1953–57–59–61–63–65–67–69, non-playing captain 1973. Runner-up 1960 World Cup (with Harry Weetman).

Has easy, three-quarter backswing and, when swinging smoothly, is still a fine player. With a short backswing, you must swing slowly; the shorter the backswing, the slower it must be, otherwise you lose rhythm and can go off line.

**Hale Irwin**

Born 3.6.45, Joplin, Missouri, USA. Turned pro 1968. With four holes to play in 1970 Los Angeles Open, led Casper by two strokes, earning latter's forecast that he would become a first-time winner, but lost on a sudden-death play off and had to wait for 1971 Heritage Classic for first Tour victory. Made his big breakthrough in 1974, winning US Open and Piccadilly World Match Play. Best Tour year 1974, $152,529 (7th). US World Cup team 1974, finishing third in both individual and team events.

Comparing his former sport, American football, with golf, says: 'In football you can get rid of your emotions, you can tackle somebody hard, for instance, but in golf the pressure keeps building. You have to control your emotions and that's sometimes hard.'

**Tony Jacklin**

Born 7.7.44, Scunthorpe, Lincs. Britain's most successful post-war golfer. Started at age of nine and turned pro 1962. Graduated from US qualifying school 1967, joined Tour and won the 1968 Jacksonville Open with record 15-under-par 273. Won British Open 1969 and US Open 1970, becoming only British player to hold both titles concurrently. Won Italian Open 1973, Scandinavian Open and Texaco Pro-Am 1974. British Ryder Cup team 1967–69–71–73. Represented England in World Cup 1966–70–71–72. Best US Tour year 1970, $87,559 (20th). Moved to Jersey for tax reasons early in 1975.

Rather quick action sometimes gets him into trouble, especially when he tries to hit the ball too far too quickly and gets outside the line of flight from the top of the backswing. Very good putter and bunker player. If his backswing appears smooth and slow, he is in top form.

**Grier Jones** *(below)*
Born 6.5.46, Wichita, Kansas, USA. Turned pro 1968 and won first two Tour events in 1972, grossing $140,177 winnings. In the previous year he had been 72nd on the money list, then decided that his approach to the game had been negative, set himself the target of getting back in the top 60 and ended the 1972 season in fourth place. Runner-up in two 1974 Tour events.

**George Knudson** *(left)*
Born 28.6.37, Winnipeg, Canada. Turned pro 1958 and has won 12 events on US Tour. Won individual World Cup title 1966, after tie with Hideo Sugimoto (Japan) and the team event (with Al Balding) in 1968. Best Tour year 1972, $74,366 (30th).

Trademark the dark glasses, without which he can hardly see. Uses weightlifting and calisthenic exercises to boost his weight. Is rated one of the game's finest shot-makers by fellow professionals.

**Cobie Legrange**
Born 22.10.42, Boksburg, S. Africa. Turned pro 1963. Won S. African Dunlop Masters 1964–69. Spent more than 300 days in 1963 perfecting a new swing, after describing his former one as 'mechanical, without rhythm and with a loop at the top that caused me to block the ball away with consequent loss of power'.

**John Lister**
Born 3.9.47, Temuka, New Zealand. Graduated from US PGA qualifying school 1970. Has played three World Cups for New Zealand, finishing third (with Bob Charles) in the 1971 team event.

Well over 6ft and 13 stone, hits the ball great distances and is a fine putter. Not a particularly long backswing, but a good, solid follow through and uses his legs throughout the swing. Has the characteristics of all long hitters.

**Gene Littler**

Born 21.7.30, San Diego, Calif., USA. Won US Amateur 1953 and San Diego Open 1954 while still amateur, turning pro in the same month as the latter event and finishing second in the US Open later the same year. Won US Open 1961, Tournament of Champions 1955–56–57, Canadian Open 1965. Tour wins total 26, including 1973 St Louis Children's Hospital Classic, 16 months after undergoing an operation for cancer. Won Taiheiho Masters, Japan, 1974, Bing Crosby National Pro-Am 1975. US Ryder Cup team 1961–63–65–67–69–71. Best Tour year 1969, $112,737 (6th).

Sometimes called 'Gene the Machine', is one of the great stylists, neat and elegant. Not a big man, but has fine poise and balance and does not waste time. Excellent short game and a good putter.

**Liang-Huan Lu**

Born Taipeh, Taiwan, 1937. Began playing golf at eight and turned pro 1955. Joining Far East circuit, won the 1959 Hong Kong Open, 1965 Philippines Open and 1966 China (Taiwan) Open, but became internationally famous at 1971 British Open, endearing himself to the crowd and television viewers with his hat-raising acknowledgment of applause, earning nickname 'Mr Lu' and finishing second to Lee Trevino. Won French Open 1971, World Cup team event (with Hsieh Min-Nan) 1972, third team and joint third individual 1973, fourth team and joint fourth individual 1974.

A very easy player, a small man, hits the ball sweetly and had a great match with Jack Nicklaus at 1971 Piccadilly World Match Play Championship.

**John Mahaffey**

Born 9.5.48, Kerrville, Texas, USA. After a successful amateur career, turned pro 1971 and was spotted as a player of great potential by Ben Hogan, who obtained him a special invitation to play the Colonial National event, in which he tied for 12th place. He earned $57,779 for 39th place on the money list in 1972, his first full year on the Tour, and boosted this to $112,536 and 12th place in 1973, when he won the Sahara Invitational tournament. Although without a Tour win in 1974, he was 16th on money list with $122,189.

**Graham Marsh**

Born 14.1.44, Kalgoorlie, Australia. Turned pro 1968, after being runner-up in previous year's Australian Amateur championship. Won Swiss Open 1970–72, New Zealand Spalding Masters 1971, Indian Open 1971, German Open 1972, Scottish Open 1973. Runner-up Piccadilly World Match Play 1973 and a prolific money-winner on the Far East circuit. Brother of Australian Test wicket-keeper, Rodney Marsh.

**Johnny Miller**
Born 29.4.47, San Francisco, Calif., USA. Won USGA junior title 1964 and Californian Amateur 1968. Graduated to Tour 1969 and has been protégé of his Mormon co-religionist, Billy Casper. His third round of 61 in Phoenix Open was lowest on 1970 Tour and his first win on it, the Southern Open, came in following year. Really arrived by winning 1973 US Open, with a final round of 63, then finished joint second in British Open. Winner World Cup team (with Jack Nicklaus) and individual 1973. In 1974 won eight Tour events – including the first three – and collected a record $353,021 prize money, to finish US PGA Player of the Year. Started 1975 with three wins in first five Tour events.

Lanky, 6ft 2in., has upright swing and flights the ball high. Owes much to Casper's advice, particularly on 'playing the percentages'.

**Hsieh Min-Nan**
Born 1942. From Taiwan and now based in Japan. Made his big breakthrough in 1972, after being rated Taiwan's second best player, behind Liang-Huan Lu. In that year he won the Thailand Open, was leading Asian player in the continent's Order of Merit Grand Prix and finished, in Melbourne, by winning the individual and team (with Liang-Huan Lu) World Cup titles. He was also leading Asian player in the British Open 1972.

**Bobby Mitchell**
Born 23.2.43, Chatham, Virginia, USA. Turned pro at 15 in 1958, but did not join Tour until 1966 and proved his assertion that it took a player two years on it to know if he could make the grade by boosting his winnings from $3,662 in 1967 to $20,699 in 1968. Has won two Tour events, including Tournament of Champions in 1972, his best year with winnings of $113,719 (11th).

**Orville Moody**

Born 9.12.33, Chickasha, Oklahoma, USA. Left US Army to turn pro 1967, scoring first tournament win in 1969 US Open and winning World Series in same year. Won World Cup team event (with Lee Trevino) 1969, Moroccan Open 1971. USPGA Player of Year 1969. Best Tour year 1969, $79,176.

Super-patriot, usually wears red, white and blue colours. Has never taken golfing lesson and spends little time in practice. Very good in bad conditions, where he can keep the ball low. Won US Open using his cack-handed putting style, right hand at the top of the shaft.

**Bob Murphy**

Born 14.2.43, Brooklyn, New York, USA. US Amateur champion 1965. Turned pro 1967, after playing in US Walker Cup team and won first two of three Tour events to date in 1968. In first six seasons on Tour collected $105,595, $56,526, $120,639, $75,301, $83,259 and $93,442 respectively. Missed much of 1974 season with thumb injury, but returned to old form by winning 1975 Jackie Gleason Inverary Classic.

At 5ft 10in. and weighing nearly 15½ stone, says: 'Just because a guy is fat doesn't make him lazy or slovenly' and, of his pattern of fading the ball, 'You have to get the ball on the green, then get it into the hole – and it doesn't matter how you look while doing it.'

**Kel Nagle**

Born 21.12.20, Australia. Turned pro 1939. Won British Open 1960–64, Canadian Open 1964, New Zealand Open 1957–58–62–64–67–68–69. World Cup team winner 1954–59 and runner-up 1955–61 (all with Peter Thomson).

Fine, straight hitter of the ball. Very simple swing, three-quarter back and straight through. Still, at 54, good competitor and great front runner. Very good touch round greens, with everything chopped off short – like driving in a nail, rather than swinging an axe. This short, decisive, punchy movement flows right through his game.

**Jack Newton**

Born 30.1.50, Sydney, Australia. A qualified physical education teacher, he made his mark on first tour of Britain and Europe in 1972 by winning the Benson and Hedges stroke-play and Dutch Open. Won Benson and Hedges match play 1974. An outspoken defender of Australian golf standards, says the media of that country give too much prominence to US players.

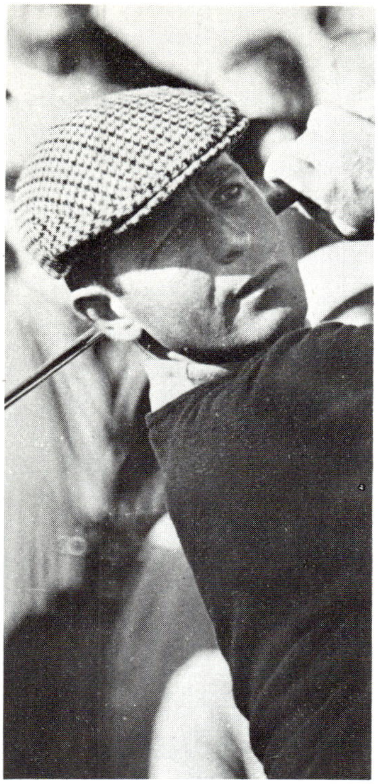

**Bobby Nichols**
Born 14.4.36, Louisville, Kentucky, USA. Critically injured in 1952 car crash, was voted the Ben Hogan award ten years later for his determination in making a recovery and playing winning golf. Turned pro 1959, joined Tour in following year and scored first two of 12 wins on it – including 1964 US PGA – during 1962. Won Canadian and Andy Williams–San Diego Opens 1974. US Ryder Cup team 1967. Best Tour year 1974, $124,747 (14th).

Fine swing and excellent putting touch around the green. High backswing, with arms extended almost to their fullest extent and big shoulder turn, help him to be one of the world's longest hitters.

**Jack Nicklaus**
Born 21.1.40, Columbus, Ohio, USA. Leading money-winner on the US Tour for the sixth time in 1973 ($308,362) – has topped $100,000 in every season but his first, 1962, and never been lower than fourth on money list. US Amateur champion 1959–61, turned pro 1961 and won three Tour events, including US Open, in 1962. Won US Open again 1967–72, British Open 1966–70, US PGA 1963–71–73. US Masters 1963–65–66–72, and is one of only four players to achieve 'Grand Slam'. The 1973 US PGA brought his number of major titles to 14, breaking a record held since 1930 by Bobby Jones. Fifty-three Tour wins 1962–74 and other titles include World Series 1962–63–67–70, Australian Open 1964–68–71; World Cup team 1963–64–66–67 (with Arnold Palmer), 1971 (with Lee Trevino), 1973 (with John Miller), individual 1963–64–71; Piccadilly World Match Play 1970. US PGA Player of the Year 1967–72. US Ryder Cup team 1969–71–73.

Slow, deliberate player. Stands behind the ball, gets a good view to the target, then settles himself, never hurrying. Slow, deliberate backswing, with club lifted into the air, rather than the shoulders turning it. Powerful legs help him as he comes down and through the ball. Arguably the greatest player of all time.

**Christy O'Connor Snr** *(left)*

Born 21.12.24, Galway, Eire. Consistent money-winner on British circuit since 1959, ending 1970 with £31,352, thanks mainly to £25,000 first prize in John Player Classic. Won World (then Canada) Cup team event (with Harry Bradshaw) 1958, losing individual title after play-off with Angel Miguel (Spain). Awarded Harry Vardon Trophy 1961–62. Regular member of British Ryder Cup team since 1955.

Has free flowing swing and is master of recovery shots from rough. It is a joy to see him using a 4 wood out of heavy rough or pitching over bunkers. Has holed many good putts, but never been consistent in this department, otherwise could have ranked with Palmer, Nicklaus and Player.

**Peter Oosterhuis** *(above)*

Born 3.5.48, London. Won British Youths title 1966. Walker Cup team 1967. Turned pro 1968. Wins include French Open 1973–74, Italian and El Paraiso Opens 1974. Headed PGA Order of Merit 1971–72–73–74. Joint 3rd 1973 US Masters and led at end of third round. Britain's Ryder Cup team 1971–73, with singles wins over Arnold Palmer, Gene Littler and Gary Player. Runner-up British Open 1974 and leading money-winner PGA Tour with £32,127, also securing his player's card for 1975 US Tour.

This 6ft 5in. giant has a shortish backswing, with a little bit of a flail in it – flicking the wrist when starting the downward movement from the top of the swing. Wonderful temperament: although he gets angry with himself, he is able to control it and this, allied to a fine touch within 30 or 40 yards of the flag and on the green itself, should make him one of the world's leading players over the next few years.

**Masashi Ozaki**

Born 1948, Japan. Ozaki, six feet tall and known as 'Jumbo', reinforced his position as one of the Far East's growing group of players in world class during 1973, when his victories included the £122,500 Taiheyo Masters Tournament, after a three-hole play-off with Bert Yancey. Became first 'home' winner of Japan Open with his fifth win of 1974 – and a 7-under-par final round. Previous wins included the 1971 Japan PGA and 1972 New Zealand PGA. Runner-up World Cup individual and team (with Isao Aoki) 1974.

**Arnold Palmer**

Born 10.9.29, Latrobe, Pennsylvania, USA. First played golf when three years old and, since the late 1950s, has been most successful and popular player in the world, followed everywhere on US Tour – in which he won 61 events 1955–73 – by his personal fan club, 'Arnie's Army'. Turned pro after winning 1954 US Amateur and has been Tour's top prize-winner four times, collecting well over $1½ million. Titles include US Open 1960, US Masters 1958–60–62–64, British Open 1961–62, Canadian Open 1955, PGA team (with Jack Nicklaus) 1971, Piccadilly World Match Play 1964–67, World Cup team (with Sam Snead) 1960–62, (with Nicklaus) 1963–64–66–67, World Cup individual 1967. US Ryder Cup team 1961–63–65–67–71–73. US PGA Player of the Year 1960–62. Best Tour year 1971, $209,603.

Very strong, with probably the most powerful hands of anyone in professional golf: they fit on to the grip, making the club appear like a wand. One of the best chippers, but not a particularly good bunker player compared with, say, Gary Player. As good as anyone in world in any situation around the green requiring a delicate shot.

**Gary Player**

Born 1.11.36, Johannesburg, S. Africa. From childhood patterned his game on Ben Hogan, a policy which later helped make him, like Hogan, one of the only four players to do the 'Grand Slam' – US Open (1965), British Open (1959–68–74), US Masters (1961–74) and US PGA (1962–72). A physical fitness fanatic, strict dietician, Player turned pro in 1953. He has won 18 US Tour events and the Piccadilly World Match Play Championship five times (1965–66–68–71–73). World Cup team (with Harold Henning) and individual 1965, runner-up team and individual 1973. Won Australian Open for seventh time in 1974 – his 100th professional victory. During the 1960s he, Palmer and Nicklaus, all then managed by Mark McCormack, became known as the 'Big Three', to the annoyance of other players. Best Tour year 1969, $123,897 (5th).

Tremendously powerful arms and stands well away from the ball, giving himself plenty of room to turn. Tends to hook the ball, that is hit from right to left, but is one of the great bunker players, repeatedly saving himself with wonderful recovery shots. Superb putter: particularly on the short ones he keeps his head down, the putter is taken back perhaps just two or three inches, quite slowly, then he gives a good, firm tap, usually sending the ball into the middle of the hole. Spends hours in practice and is totally dedicated.

**Eddie Polland**
Born 10.6.47, Newcastle, Co. Down. Runner-up Irish Boys' Championship 1965. Turned pro 1966, but did not make his breakthrough until 1973, when winning the Penfold–Bournemouth tournament. Played in Britain's 1973 Ryder Cup team and for Ireland in World Cup 1973–74.

**Mason Rudolph**
Born 23.5.34, Clarksville, Tennessee, USA. Former US Junior champion. Walker Cup team 1957 and turned pro 1958. Six wins on US Tour. Ryder Cup 1971. Best Tour year 1973, $61,270.

Regained his former immaculate putting touch in 1970, thanks to a tip from Phil Rodgers.

**Juan ('Chi-Chi') Rodriguez**
Born 13.10.35, Puerto Rico. Came up the hard way as caddie in Puerto Rico. Turned pro 1960. Seven wins on US Tour with best year 1972, $113,503 (12th). US Ryder Cup team 1973.

For his size (5ft 7½in., 125lb.) hits the ball great distances. Has strong arms and hands and launches himself into the ball, hitting it as hard as he possibly can. Inelegant player, but an expert at all sorts of trouble shots around the green, whether from deep rough or buried bunkers. Great touch and finesse.

**Doug Sanders**
Born 24.6.33, Cedartown, Georgia, USA. Turned pro 1956 after winning Canadian Open as an amateur. Has since won 19 US Tour events. Colourful dresser and high liver. US Ryder Cup team 1967. Best Tour year 1972, $102,252. Out of competition for most of 1974, as a result of surgery on his right arm, but came back to play in Rest of World team at the Double Diamond Championship.

Inelegant swing goes with a wide stance and very short backswing. Aided by strong arms, hands and hips, he whips the clubhead through at a great pace. One of golf's great artists, can flight the ball either high or low and hook or fade at will.

**John Schlee**
Born 2.6.39, Kremling, Colorado, USA. Turned pro 1964, but this sparetime astrologer took eight full years on the US Tour to reach the stars, when winning the Hawaiian Open and finishing runner-up to Johnny Miller in the US Open of 1973, his best money-winning campaign with $118,017 (10th). Handicapped by back injury in 1974.

**Doug Sewell** *(left)*
Born 19.11.29, Woking, Surrey. English Amateur title 1958–60. Played in Home internationals 1956–58–59–60; Great Britain *v.* US 1957–59; *v.* World 1960; *v.* Commonwealth 1969.

Not a long hitter, but among the most accurate players in golf. A unique putting style: spreads his legs, gets right over the ball, finger down the shaft, very stiff elbows, arms and club all seem to be in one piece, fairly stiff backswing just pushes the ball through to the hole, while keeping his head very still.

**Ronnie Shade**
Born 15.10.38, Edinburgh. Scottish Amateur champion 1963–64–65–66–67. World Individual amateur champion 1966. British Walker Cup team 1961–63–65–67. Turned pro 1968. Scottish World Cup team 1970–71–72.

The 'mechanical man', looks artificial and stiff, but is very accurate with a fine short game.

**Sewsunker ('Papwa') Sewgolum**
Born Durban, South Africa, of Indian parents and now in his mid 40s. Earns his place by his great achievements, despite being victim of apartheid. Cannot read or write and taught himself golf as a boy caddie. First non-white to play South African Open (1961). Won Natal Open 1963 and 1965, when he beat Gary Player, Dutch Open 1959–60–64. Barred from 'white' competition in South Africa since 1965.

One of the few cack-handed players in the world (left hand below right, although a natural right-hander), is now possibly past his prime, but has been one of the game's greatest putters.

**Charles Sifford**

Born 3.6.23, Charlotte, North Carolina, USA. Started golf as ten-year-old caddie. Served three years in Army during World War II, turned pro 1947 and won national Negro title five times. Became first Negro to win scheduled Tour event in 1967 Hartford Open, aged 45, and has won one since. Best Tour year 1967, $47,025.

Has an awkward swing, falling away so much at the finish that he looks likely to topple over, but is a long, accurate hitter.

**Dan Sikes**

Born 7.12.30, Jacksonville, Florida, USA. A law graduate, but does not practise and says golf is a more lucrative profession. Won an army title 1955, turned pro 1960. Six wins on US Tour, with best year 1967, $111,508. US Ryder Cup team 1969.

One of the Tour's most accurate drivers, with above average length and a swing marked by a slow take-away and pronounced pause at the top. Says it was influenced by Cary Middlecoff's style.

**J. C. (Jesse) Snead**

Born 14.10.41, Hot Springs, Virginia, USA. Nephew of Sam Snead. Turned pro 1964 and joined US Tour 1968. Won two Tour events 1971, another in 1972, Andy Williams San Diego 1975, Australian Open 1973. US Ryder Cup team 1971–73. Best Tour year 1974, $164,486 (5th).

Well over 6ft in height, has delicate touch around the green. His huge forearms can smash into the ball with almost terrifying power.

**Ramon Sota**

Born 23.4.38, Pedreña, Spain. Turned pro 1957. Has won Portuguese Open three times, Dutch Open twice and French, Spanish, Italian, Brazilian and Puerto Rican Opens each once. Has represented Spain eight times in World Cup, finishing team runner-up with S. Miguel 1963 and A. Miguel 1965. Among top 13 in British Open three times.

Spain's answer to Brian Huggett: bigger in build, but has many of the Welshman's mannerisms, plus his fierce determination.

**Ken Still** *(left)*

Born 12.2.35, Tacoma, Washington, USA. Turned pro 1953, two years after an uncle had awakened his interest in golf by persuading him to earn holiday money as a caddie. Joined Tour 1960 and has won three events on it, with best year 1969, $72,514. US Ryder Cup team 1969.

Enthusiastic and popular with playing partners, for whom he acts as unofficial cheerleader.

**Hideyo Sugimoto**

Born 13.2.38, Shizuoka, Japan. Turned pro 1959. Won Japan Open 1964–69, All Japan Best Ball 1969–70, Japan Golf Series 1970. Japanese World Cup team 1965–66–67, individual runner-up 1966, after play-off with George Knudson.

**Dave Stockton**

Born 2.11.41, San Bernardino, Calif., USA. Taught golf by his ex-pro father, Gail. Turned pro 1964 and has won ten Tour events, including 1970 US PGA and three in 1974. Runner-up 1974 US Masters. US Ryder Cup team 1971. Best Tour year 1974, $155,105 (6th).

Very quick player, reminiscent of Harry Bradshaw. Has a wide stance when putting, stands well over the ball and hits it solidly.

**Leonard Thompson**

Born 1.1.47, Laurinburg, N. Carolina, USA. Like Arnold Palmer and Lanny Wadkins, was a member of the Wake Forest University golf team. A big man – 6ft 2in. and over 14 st. – Thompson plays with great determination and has learned to curb a hot temper. He turned pro 1970, finished 25th on the 1973 money list with $91,158 and won his first Tour event, the Jackie Gleason Classic, in 1974, finishing the year with $122,349 (15th).

**Peter Thomson**

Born 23.8.29, Melbourne, Australia. Turned pro 1949. Won British Open 1954–55–56–58–65, runner-up 1952–57. Won New Zealand Open nine times. Won World Cup team 1954–59, runner-up 1955–61 (all with Kel Nagle); individual runner-up 1959, after the tie with S. Leonard (Canada).

Apart from Gene Littler and Bobby Locke, probably has had the best rhythm and balance the world has ever seen. A simple style, rather a strong left-hand grip, showing three and a half knuckles, he gives the impression of holding the club very lightly. This, allied to lateral movement in the swing, sometimes leads him into trouble. Never seems restricted in the length of his backswing. Even on the shortest putts, the putter is taken well away from the ball, with very little follow through.

**Peter Townsend**

Born 16.9.46, Cambridge. British Boys champion 1962–64, Youth champion and Walker Cup team 1965. Turned pro 1966 and won Dutch Open 1967, aged 20. Won Venezuelan Open 1969. British Ryder Cup team 1969–71. English World Cup team 1974.

**Lee Trevino** *(below)*

Born 1.12.39, Dallas, Texas, USA, of Mexican parents. Learned golf in US Marine Corps and turned pro 1960. Joined Tour 1966, winning $600, but collected well over a million dollars in next seven years, finishing top money-winner in 1970; second, with a personal record of $231,202, in 1971 and again, with $214,805, in 1972, and fourth in 1973 and 1974. Won US Open 1968 and in 1971, when he went on to collect Canadian and British Open titles within following three weeks. Won British Open 1972, US PGA, World Series and Greater New Orleans Open 1974. World Cup team winner (with Orville Moody) 1969 and (with Jack Nicklaus) 1971; individual winner 1969; team runner-up (with Julius Boros) 1968. US PGA Player of the Year 1971. US Ryder Cup team 1969–71–73. Florida Citrus Open 1975 his 18th Tour win.

Stands far away from the ball at the address position, has a very slow swing, round the corner, instead of up and down. Dips his head some nine inches as he comes into the ball. He stalks around the green, tugging at his peaked cap and the collar of his shirt, then walks straight up to the ball, one or two quick practice swings and it's on its way, usually into the hole.

**Lanny Wadkins**
Born 5.12.49, Richmond, Virginia, USA. First broke 80 when ten years old, won National Pee Wee title three years later and American Amateur in 1970, turning pro the following year. Won 1972 Sahara Open, finishing tenth in US money list with $116,616, a record for a first-year Tourist. In 1973 he was fifth, with $200,455. Won two Tour events in 1973 and is one of America's most promising young players.

**Art Wall** *(left)*
Born 25.11.23, Honesdale, Pennsylvania, USA. Turned pro and joined US Tour 1949, on graduating from university. Won US Masters and named American Player of the Year 1959, with top Tour winnings of $53,167. Has won 13 Tour events and more than half-a-million dollars prize money, with another eight victories on Caribbean Tour. Hit his 41st hole-in-one during 1973. US Ryder Cup team 1957–59–61.

Probably the game's greatest money-winner before the Palmer–Nicklaus era. Changes to left hand below right for short putts. Uses five-finger 'baseball' grip – and says he did not know there was any other when he learned to play.

**Tom Watson**
Born 4.9.49, Kansas City, Missouri, USA. Started playing golf at age of six, under guidance of his scratch handicap father, and went on to win the Missouri Amateur title four times, before turning pro in 1971, the year of his graduation in psychology at Stanford University.

He finished 79th on the Tour money list in 1972, 35th in 1973 and 10th, with $135,474, in 1974, when he won the Western Open.

**Tom Weiskopf** *(left)*
Born 9.11.42, Massillon, Ohio, USA. Father (plus two handicap) and mother (scratch) both good golfers. He first played golf when 15, scoring 93 in his first round, reducing this to the high 70s within three months. First two Tour wins in 1968, when he finished third in the US money list, two more in 1971, another – plus the Piccadilly World Match Play – in 1972 and the big breakthrough in 1973, when he took the British and Canadian Opens, three Tour events, the World Series and South African PGA. US World Cup team 1972. US Ryder Cup team 1973. Third on US money list 1973, with $245,463.

A well-built 6ft 3in., one of the longest hitters and best putters in American golf, with enormous confidence in his swing and general ability.

**Bert Yancey** *(above)*
Born 6.8.38, Chipley, Florida, USA. Former West Point cadet, turned pro 1961 following nervous breakdown and medical discharge from Army. Won first three of his seven Tour victories in 1966. Twice runner-up in Pacific Masters. Best Tour year 1974, $84,692.

A perfectionist, who believes mental approach is 90 per cent of success, he looks so good, but has achieved comparatively little. Comparing Yancey and Trevino is like comparing Denis Compton with Sir Leonard Hutton: completely different, both highly effective.

**Haruo Yasuda**
Born 19.1.43, Tokyo, Japan. Passed his pro test exam when 18 and for a long time was known as 'the permanent runner-up', but a series of wins, including the Manila Open, brought him into the limelight in 1969. Japanese World Cup team 1969–70–71, runner-up (with T. Kono) 1969. Won Singapore Open 1971.

Quick-tempered and temperamental, he is a long hitter for a relatively small man, thanks to excellent timing and a long, flowing swing, in which he uses his legs to help create great clubhead speed.

# 5 Glossary of terms

*Tony Jacklin*

**Ace** A hole in one.

**Address** Putting oneself into position to hit the ball.

**Albatross** A hole achieved in three strokes under par.

**Air shot** When the clubhead and ball fail to make contact during a shot. The stroke still counts towards the player's score.

**Arc** (of the swing) The groove or movement of the clubhead while playing a shot.

**Ball** In Britain the size of the ball must be not less than 1·620 inches in diameter. In the US the size must be not less than 1·680 inches in diameter. The US size has been compulsory in British PGA tournaments since 1968 and in the British Open in 1974 and 1975.

**Better ball** A competition in which two partners play as a team, the better score of either counting.

**Birdie** A hole achieved in one stroke under par.

**Blaster** A deep-faced club used for recovery shots from bunkers and other hazards.

**Blind** (hole or shot) A blind hole is when the green cannot be seen from the tee. A blind shot is when trees or a rise in ground prevent the player seeing where he intends to hit the ball.

**Bogey** Generally this is regarded as the score for each hole which should be taken by a scratch golfer in his or her normal form in average playing conditions. It is not the same as par. In the US the term 'bogey' means one stroke over par. Usually in Britain the bogey of an 18-hole course is one or two strokes above par, which is a stricter form of defining the test offered by a course. In golf there are bogey competitions in which the golfer plays against the bogey of each hole.

**Borrow** To take advantage of the slope on a green. If, for instance, there was a right-to-left slope on the green between your ball and the hole, the putt would be hit so that the ball would first go to the right and then, with the aid of the slope, hopefully reach the hole. Borrow can also mean the slope of the green between ball and hole.

**Brassie** The equivalent club today is the No. 2 wood.

**Bunker** A hazard filled with sand. Bunkers are sited at various points on and at the sides of the fairway and are usually to be found beside greens to trap poor shots.

**Bye** The number of holes remaining to be played at the end of a match, when one player or team has been beaten. In friendly games there are often wagers on who can win the bye, or remaining hole(s).

**Caddie** Someone who carries clubs for a golfer. Derived from an old French word, 'cadet', meaning young boy. Brought to Scotland by French followers of Mary Queen of Scots.

**Caddie cart** A two-wheeled cart for carrying clubs, etc., and pulled by hand. Also known as trolley. Electric trolleys, motorised and guided like milk floats, originated in the US and are gaining popularity in Britain.

**Casual water** Water forming pools on courses after heavy rain. If the ball goes into such a pool, it can be lifted without penalty. If the accumulation of water is not immediately apparent, but is seen by the golfer as he takes up his stance, a lift and drop is still permissible, though this sometimes causes controversy.

**Chip** A short, lofted shot to the green.

**Cleaning the ball** A ball lying on the putting green may be lifted and cleaned and replaced on the same spot.

**Clubs** A player shall start a round with not more than fourteen clubs. If the player starts with fewer than fourteen the number carried may be added to without causing undue delay. A club which has been broken may be replaced. Clubs cannot be borrowed from any other person playing on the course. Partners may share clubs provided the total number carried does not exceed fourteen.

**Concede** A hole is conceded when one player has taken so many strokes that it is impossible for him to win it. He can pick up his ball, thus indicating that he has conceded the hole to his opponent, or tell the latter of his intention.

**Course** The ground over which golf is played. Courses are usually made up of 18 holes, but can be of nine, which may be played over twice for 18-hole games. Courses consist of teeing grounds, fairways, greens, rough and other hazards, some of which are man-made and others natural. The number of holes varied on early courses and there is no special reason why 18 became general.

**Dead** When the ball stops so near a hole that to miss a putt would be virtually impossible. There is no specific distance for this, but the criterion is usually a matter of a few inches.

**Divot** The piece of turf cut out by the club striking a ball a descending blow. Good players take huge divots, but these must always be replaced and trodden down, to avoid damage to the course. Loose divots attract crows, who carry them off.

**Dogleg** A hole which turns to left or right, with a hazardous area in the bend.

**Dormie (or Dormy)** When a golfer, or a golfer and his partner are as many holes up in match play as there remain to be played in a round, e.g. if one player or side were four holes up and four holes remained to be played, he or they would be dormie. The opponent(s) could not then win the round, but only halve it by winning all the remaining holes.

**Draw** To put spin on the ball when making a stroke, so that it comes in from right to left.

**Drive** A full shot from the tee, when distance is needed.

**Eagle** A score of two strokes better than par.

**Fairway** The cut or mown part of the course, between teeing ground and green.

**Flagstick** A movable pole or post with flag or bunting attached placed in the hole to show its position. A player may have the flagstick attended, removed or held up to indicate the position of the hole. This may be done only on the authority of the player before he plays his stroke. Under Rule 34 there are penalties for a ball striking the flagstick.

**Fluff (or Duff)** A shot in which the club hits the ground, rather than the ball, resulting in the latter going only a short distance.

**Follow through** The part of the swing in which the arms move on, after the ball has been hit.

**Fore** The shout of warning to anyone on the course that a ball is going in their direction.

**Forward press** Pressing the hands forward before hitting the ball, to give more spring to the movement.

**Four-ball** A match in which the pairs play as teams, with the lower score of the two partners counting at each hole.

**Foursomes** Matches between two teams of two players, each team playing with one ball, the partners having alternate strokes and driving at alternate holes. Known in US as a 'Scotch foursome'.

**Green** Used to describe the entire course in the early days of golf, but now applied only to the putting surface of each hole.

**Greensome** A form of foursomes, in which all four players drive, then each team can choose which ball to use for the rest of each hole. Popular at many clubs.

**Ground under repair** Ground which has been repaired by greenkeepers and almost always marked by a notice. Balls coming to rest on such ground can be lifted and dropped off it without penalty.

**Halved** A hole or match is halved when opponents are level, either in relation to strokes taken at the hole in question, or when they are level at the end of a match.

**Handicap** After joining a club, all golfers are given handicaps, based on scores returned after a few rounds. The usual limit for men is 18 (sometimes 24) and for women 36.

**Hanging lie** When the ball is lying on a downward slope, often in long grass or heather.

**Hazard** Any permanent obstacle on the course (e.g. bunkers, streams, etc.).

**Head** That part of the club with which the ball is struck. Heads are made of wood, a synthetic substance, or, in the case of irons, iron.

**Hole** The orifice on the green into which the ball is played. It is $4\frac{1}{4}$ inches in diameter and at least 4 inches deep. To avoid too much traffic on one part of the green the situation of the hole is changed frequently and in major tournaments often after every round.

**Hole in one** When the ball goes into the hole from the tee.

**Holing-out** Getting the ball into the hole. Sometimes used to indicate that a player has holed in a stated number of strokes at a given hole.

**Honour** The preference given the player who drives first. The honour of the first tee has to be agreed, but at subsequent holes it goes to the player with the lower score at the previous hole.

**Hook** A stroke in which the ball moves to the left in the air (or to the right for a left-handed player).

**Identification** Making certain that the ball about to be played belongs to the player in question. Except in very special circumstances, where no name is visible, the ball must not be lifted.

**In** The second nine holes in a course of 18.

**Irons** As the name suggests, clubs with the heads made of iron. Irons range from No. 1, which has very little loft, to the No. 9, or wedge or blaster, which has a great deal of loft, i.e. the face is set well back. The low-numbered irons are used for longer shots from the fairway, the higher for short shots and recovery shots, where varying degrees of height are needed. The No. 1 iron is now rarely used, because it is difficult to play; it is usually substituted by a wooden club.

**Ladies' tee** The teeing ground used by women players and almost always some distance in front of that used by men. Ladies' handicaps are calculated from these tees.

**Lie** The position in which a ball comes to rest after it has been played.

**Lift and drop** When, for some reason, it is impossible to play the ball from the position in which it lies and it has to be lifted and dropped. There is usually, though not always, a penalty for lifting and dropping and the rule book must be consulted to find governing circumstances.

**Like as we lie** The situation in which each player has played the same number of strokes for a hole. 'Playing the like' is to play a stroke which brings one's score for a hole to the same number of strokes as one's opponent at that point.

**Links** Golf was first played at the seaside and courses there became known as links, the term given to ground beside the sea.

**Local rules** All clubs have their own sets of 'local rules', covering points arising from conditions on their particular courses. These are in addition to the rules of golf laid down in most countries by the Royal and Ancient Club of St Andrews and in the United States by the US Golf Association.

**Loft** The angle at which the clubhead lies in relation to the shaft. Loft increases in degree from the straight-faced driver to the wedge, or No. 9 iron. Putters are straight-faced (see 'Woods' and 'Irons').

**Lost ball** When a ball is lost in play, golfers are allowed five minutes to look for it, after which they must play another ball according to the rules.

**Mashie** A short-faced lofted club popularised by J. H. Taylor. The modern counterpart is the No. 5 or 6 iron.

**Mashie niblick** A club with more loft than the mashie and not as much loft as a niblick. Equivalent to the No. 7 iron of today.

**Match play** Where the result of a match is decided by the player(s) who have won the greater number of holes. For example, a player in a match can be three holes up, with two to play and then be in a winning position.

**Medal play** Medal or stroke play competition is decided by the number of strokes taken during the round, not the number of holes won. Monthly medal competitions are a feature of all golf clubs.

**Obstructions** Objects, movable or immovable, which prevent the playing of a shot.

**Out** The first nine holes in a course of 18.

**Out of bounds** When the ball is played outside the limits of the course or hole, thus incurring the penalty indicated by the rules.

**Outside agency** A person or animal who removes a ball after it has been played. If the ball is seen to be so removed after it has come to rest, no penalty is incurred.

**Par** Par, as laid down by the Standard Scratch Score and Handicapping scheme prepared by the Council of National Golf Unions, is 'the score in which a first-class player should play a hole in summer conditions'. Par for each hole is fixed as follows: holes of 250 yards and under, par 3; holes between 251 and 475 yards, par 4; holes of 476 yards or more, par 5. The term Par has replaced Bogey.

**Partner** The person with whom one plays golf.

**Penalty** When a shot is played into a lie from which it is unplayable, or out of bounds, a penalty is incurred according to the rules of the game. It can also be incurred for infringing the rules.

**Pitch** A short-distance shot to the green, played for the ball to travel high, with enough backspin imparted and the angle of descent right for it to come to rest near where it lands.

**Playing the odd** When a player, having been on level terms, plays a further shot, to make his score one more than his opponent.

**Playing out of turn** If a golfer plays out of turn, on either tee or fairway, his opponent may require the ball to be called back and the shot replayed. The player further from the ball should always play first.

**Pin high** When, after a shot played to the green, the ball finishes exactly level with the flag.

**Pull** To send the ball in a straight line to the left side of the course.

**Push, or push out** To send the ball in a straight line to the right side of the course.

**Putt** The stroke used on the putting surface of the course, i.e. the greens. The club used for the stroke is a putter. Most popular type is the centre-shafted putter, which has the shaft joining the head in the centre, not at one end.

**Round** Playing all the holes on the course, usually 18 holes, but in the cases of nine-hole courses, nine holes. Generally, the term means 18 holes.

**Rub of the green** Any unfortunate happening for which only fate is responsible.

**Rules of Golf** The rules under which golf is played. In Britain and in most parts of the world the game is played under the rules of the Royal and Ancient Club of St Andrews. In the US the rules are formulated by the United States Golf Association.

**Sand wedge** One of the clubs used for recovery shots from bunkers.

**Scorecard** The card taken out and marked by golfers during a round. It has to be filled in by a golfer's partner, checked and signed by both players.

**Single** A match in which two players are opposed to each other, or in medal play are playing together.

**Slice** When the ball curves to the right as a result of clockwise spin having been imparted to the ball.

**Slot** To hole out.

**Spoon** The old name for a No. 3 wood.

**Square** When the clubface is facing the target at impact. At the top of the swing the club is neither pointing to the ground nor towards the sky. The word 'square' can also be used to describe a game in which players are level. A square stance is when both feet, both hips and both shoulders are aligned to the intended flight of the ball.

**Stableford** A system for competition invented by Dr Frank Stableford, in which points are scored for the number of strokes taken at each hole. One point is scored for a hole done in one shot over bogey, two points for equalling bogey, three points for one less than bogey and so on. No points are awarded for a hole done in more than one over bogey. A player's club handicap is used in the system.

**Standard scratch score** See 'Par'.

**Stroke** The hitting of the ball during the club swing.

**Stroke competition** See 'Medal play'.

**Tee** The wooden or plastic peg on which the ball is placed before driving off. In the old days, tees were merely little piles of sand. Tee is also used to describe the teeing ground.

**Teeing ground** The part of the course used for driving from – a rectangular space with at least two club lengths to the rear of the two tee markers.

**Tee markers** Metal or plastic objects used to mark the forward limit of the teeing ground.

**Tee-pegs** See 'Tee'.

**Three-ball** A match in which three players are involved, each playing his own ball.

**Threesome** A match in which three players are involved. One plays against the other two, who play alternate shots with the one ball.

**Tie** A team match (involving several golfers on each side) which finishes level.

**Through the green** The situation which arises when a golfer has played a shot which is too strong and the ball has gone over the green. It is also used in the rules for the whole area of the course, except the teeing ground and putting green of the hole being played and all hazards on the course.

**Trap** Another name for a bunker.

**Trolley** See 'Caddie cart'.

**Unplayable ball** When the ball lies in such a position that it is impossible to hit it. It has then to be lifted and dropped in accordance with the rules.

**Waggle** The movement of the clubhead over the ball before making a shot.

**Wedge** The modern, deep-faced club with a broad sole for playing a high shot or pitch to the green, often with spin imparted to the ball.

**Winter rules** Rules for play during months when the course is wet. Winter rules entail rolling over the ball with the clubhead to ensure a better lie and thus lessen damage to the turf. This can also be called a 'preferred lie'. Winter rules can also permit cleaning the ball.

**Woods** The clubs which, as the name indicates, have heads made of wood, although now many are made of synthetic materials. A set of clubs usually includes four woods: the driver, for use off the tee; the No. 2 wood, for long fairway shots; the No. 3 wood, for fairway shots not quite as long and for playing out of good lies in the rough; and the No. 4 wood, usually used for not good lies on the fairway or for playing out of long grass. The woods are lofted in the same way as the irons. The driver has little or no loft, the No. 2 more loft, the No. 3 even more, and the No. 4 is the most lofted wood.

*Jack Nicklaus holes a bunker shot at the 16th hole during the 1st round of the 1973 British Open*

# 6 The winners

## British Open

| *year* | *winner (GB unless otherwise stated)* | *score* | *venue* |
|---|---|---|---|
| 1860 | W. Park | | Prestwick |
| 1861–2 | Tom Morris, sen. | | Prestwick |
| 1863 | W. Park | | Prestwick |
| 1864 | Tom Morris, sen. | | Prestwick |
| 1865 | A. Strath | | Prestwick |
| 1866 | W. Park | | Prestwick |
| 1867 | Tom Morris, sen. | | Prestwick |
| 1868–70 | Tom Morris, jun. | | Prestwick |
| 1871 | No competition. The present Cup was first competed for in | | |
| 1872 | Tom Morris, jun. | | Prestwick |
| 1873 | Tom Kidd | | St Andrews |
| 1874 | Mungo Park | | Musselburgh |
| 1875 | Willie Park | | Prestwick |
| 1876 | Bob Martin | | St Andrews |
| 1877 | Jamie Anderson | | Musselburgh |
| 1878 | Jamie Anderson | | Prestwick |
| 1879 | Jamie Anderson | | St Andrews |
| 1880 | Bob Ferguson | | Musselburgh |
| 1881 | Bob Ferguson | | Prestwick |
| 1882 | Bob Ferguson | | St Andrews |
| 1883 | *W. Fernie | | Musselburgh |
| 1884 | Jack Simpson | | Prestwick |
| 1885 | Bob Martin | | St Andrews |
| 1886 | D. Brown | | Musselburgh |
| 1887 | W. Park, jun. | | Prestwick |
| 1888 | Jack Burns | | St Andrews |
| 1889 | *W. Park, jun. | | Musselburgh |
| 1890 | †John Ball | | Prestwick |
| 1891 | Hugh Kirkcaldy | | St Andrews |
| | After 1891 the competition was extended to its present 72 holes. | | |
| 1892 | †H. H. Hilton | 305 | Muirfield |
| 1893 | W. Auchterlonie | 322 | Prestwick |
| 1894 | J. H. Taylor | 326 | Sandwich |
| 1895 | J. H. Taylor | 322 | St Andrews |
| 1896 | *H. Vardon | 316 | Muirfield |
| 1897 | †H. H. Hilton | 314 | Hoylake |
| 1898 | H. Vardon | 307 | Prestwick |
| 1899 | H. Vardon | 310 | Sandwich |
| 1900 | J. H. Taylor | 309 | St Andrews |
| 1901 | James Braid | 309 | Muirfield |
| 1902 | Alex Herd | 307 | Hoylake |
| 1903 | H. Vardon | 300 | Prestwick |
| 1904 | Jack White | 296 | Sandwich |
| 1905 | James Braid | 318 | St Andrews |
| 1906 | James Braid | 300 | Muirfield |
| 1907 | Arnaud Massy (F) | 312 | Hoylake |
| 1908 | James Braid | 291 | Prestwick |
| 1909 | J. H. Taylor | 295 | Deal |
| 1910 | James Braid | 299 | St Andrews |
| 1911 | *Harry Vardon | 303 | Sandwich |
| 1912 | E. Ray | 295 | Muirfield |

*after play-off
†amateur

**British Open (cont.)**

| *year* | *winner (GB unless otherwise stated)* | *score* | *venue* |
|---|---|---|---|
| 1913 | J. H. Taylor | 304 | Hoylake |
| 1914 | Harry Vardon | 306 | Prestwick |
| 1915–19 | No competition. | | |
| 1920 | George Duncan | 303 | Deal |
| 1921 | *Jock Hutchison (US) | 296 | St Andrews |
| 1922 | Walter Hagen (US) | 300 | Sandwich |
| 1923 | A. G. Havers | 295 | Troon |
| 1924 | Walter Hagen (US) | 301 | Hoylake |
| 1925 | Jim Barnes (US) | 300 | Prestwick |
| 1926 | †R. T. Jones (US) | 291 | Royal Lytham & St Annes |
| 1927 | †R. T. Jones (US) | 285 | St Andrews |
| 1928 | Walter Hagen (US) | 292 | Sandwich |
| 1929 | Walter Hagen (US) | 292 | Muirfield |
| 1930 | †R. T. Jones (US) | 291 | Hoylake |
| 1931 | T. D. Armour (US) | 296 | Carnoustie |
| 1932 | G. Sarazen (US) | 283 | Prince's, Sandwich |
| 1933 | *D Shute (US) | 292 | St Andrews |
| 1934 | T. H. Cotton | 283 | Sandwich |
| 1935 | A. Perry | 283 | Muirfield |
| 1936 | A. H. Padgham | 287 | Hoylake |
| 1937 | T. H. Cotton | 290 | Carnoustie |
| 1938 | R. A. Whitcombe | 295 | Sandwich |
| 1939 | R. Burton | 290 | St Andrews |
| 1940–45 | No competition. | | |
| 1946 | S. Snead (US) | 290 | St Andrews |
| 1947 | F. Daly | 293 | Hoylake |
| 1948 | T. H. Cotton | 284 | Muirfield |
| 1949 | *A. D. Locke (SA) | 283 | Sandwich |
| 1950 | A. D. Locke (SA) | 279 | Troon |
| 1951 | M. Faulkner | 285 | Portrush |
| 1952 | A. D. Locke (SA) | 287 | Royal Lytham |
| 1953 | B. Hogan (US) | 282 | Carnoustie |
| 1954 | P. W. Thomson (A) | 283 | Royal Birkdale |
| 1955 | P. W. Thomson (A) | 281 | St Andrews |
| 1956 | P. W. Thomson (A) | 286 | Hoylake |
| 1957 | A. D. Locke (SA) | 279 | St Andrews |
| 1958 | *P. W. Thomson (A) | 278 | Royal Lytham |
| 1959 | G. J. Player (SA) | 284 | Muirfield |
| 1960 | K. D. G. Nagle (A) | 278 | St Andrews |
| 1961 | A. Palmer (US) | 284 | Royal Birkdale |
| 1962 | A. Palmer (US) | 276 | Troon |
| 1963 | *R. J. Charles (NZ) | 277 | Royal Lytham |
| 1964 | T. Lema (US) | 279 | St Andrews |
| 1965 | P. W. Thomson (A) | 285 | Royal Birkdale |
| 1966 | J. Nicklaus (US) | 282 | Muirfield |
| 1967 | R. de Vicenzo (Arg) | 278 | Hoylake |
| 1968 | G. J. Player (SA) | 289 | Carnoustie |
| 1969 | A. Jacklin | 280 | Royal Lytham |
| 1970 | J. Nicklaus (US) | 283 | St Andrews |
| 1971 | L. Trevino (US) | 278 | Royal Birkdale |

**British Open (cont.)**

| year | winner | score | venue |
|---|---|---|---|
| 1972 | L. Trevino (US) | 278 | Muirfield |
| 1973 | T. Weiskopf (US) | 276 | Troon |
| 1974 | G. J. Player (SA) | 282 | Royal Lytham |
| 1975 | | | Carnoustie |
| 1976 | | | Royal Birkdale |

# Piccadilly

*Played at Wentworth*

| | |
|---|---|
| 1964 | A. Palmer (US) bt N. Coles (GB) 2 & 1. |
| 1965 | G. J. Player (SA) bt P. W. Thomson (A) 3 & 2. |
| 1966 | G. J. Player (SA) bt J. Nicklaus (US) 6 & 4. |
| 1967 | A. Palmer (US) bt P. W. Thomson (A) 1 up |
| 1968 | G. J. Player (SA) bt R. J. Charles (NZ) 1 up |
| 1969 | R. J. Charles (NZ) bt G. Littler (US) at 37th |
| 1970 | J. Nicklaus (US) bt L. Trevino (US) 2 & 1 |
| 1971 | G. J. Player (SA) bt J. Nicklaus (US) 5 & 4 |
| 1972 | T. Weiskopf (US) bt L. Trevino (US) 4 & 3 |
| 1973 | G. J. Player (SA) bt G. Marsh (A) at 40th |
| 1974 | H. Irwin (US) bt G. J. Player (SA) 2 & 1 |
| 1975 | |
| 1976 | |

# Double Diamond

| year | winners | venue |
|---|---|---|
| 1971 | England | S. Staffs |
| 1972 | England | Pannal |
| 1973 | Scotland | Prince's |
| 1974 | England | Gleneagles |
| 1975 | | Turnberry |
| 1976 | | |

# Ryder Cup

| year | winners | score | venue |
|---|---|---|---|
| 1927 | United States | 9–2, 1 halved | Worcester, Mass. |
| 1929 | British Isles | 6–4, 2 halved | Moortown, Leeds |
| 1931 | United States | 9–3 | Columbus, Ohio |
| 1933 | British Isles | 6–5, 1 halved | Southport & Ainsdale |
| 1935 | United States | 8–2, 2 halved | Ridgewood, N.J. |
| 1937 | United States | 7–3, 2 halved | Southport & Ainsdale |
| 1939–45 | No competition. | | |
| 1947 | United States | 11–1 | Portland, Oregon |
| 1949 | United States | 7–5 | Ganton, Scarborough |
| 1951 | United States | 9–2, 1 halved | Pinehurst, N.C. |
| 1953 | United States | 6–5, 1 halved | Wentworth |
| 1955 | United States | 8–4 | Palm Springs, Fla. |
| 1957 | British Isles | 7–4, 1 halved | Lindrick, Sheffield |
| 1959 | United States | 7–2, 3 halved | Palm Desert, Cal. |
| 1961 | United States | 13–8, 3 halved | Royal Lytham |
| 1963 | United States | 20–6, 6 halved | Atlanta, Ga. |
| 1965 | United States | 18–11, 3 halved | Royal Birkdale |
| 1967 | United States | 21–6, 5 halved | Houston, Texas |
| 1969 | Match tied | 13–13, 6 halved | Royal Birkdale |
| 1971 | United States | 16–11, 5 halved | St Louis, Mo. |
| 1973 | United States | 16–10, 6 halved | Muirfield |
| 1975 | | | Laurel Valley, Pa. |

## US Open

| *year* | *winner (US unless otherwise stated)* | *score* | *venue* |
|---|---|---|---|
| 1946 | *L. Mangrum | 284 | Canterbury, Ohio |
| 1947 | *L. Worsham | 282 | St Louis, Mo. |
| 1948 | B. Hogan | 276 | Riviera, Cal. |
| 1949 | C. Middlecoff | 286 | Medinah, Ill. |
| 1950 | *B. Hogan | 287 | Merion, Pa. |
| 1951 | B. Hogan | 287 | Oakland Hills, Mich. |
| 1952 | J. Boros | 281 | Northwood, Texas |
| 1953 | B. Hogan | 283 | Oakmont, Pa. |
| 1954 | E. Furgol | 284 | Baltusrol, N.J. |
| 1955 | *J. Fleck | 287 | Olympic, Cal. |
| 1956 | C. Middlecoff | 281 | Oak Hill, N.Y. |
| 1957 | *R. Mayer | 282 | Inverness, Ohio |
| 1958 | T. Bolt | 283 | Southern Hills, Okla. |
| 1959 | W. Casper | 282 | Winged Foot, N.Y. |
| 1960 | A. Palmer | 280 | Cherry Hills, Colo. |
| 1961 | G. Littler | 281 | Oakland Hills, Mich. |
| 1962 | *J. Nicklaus | 283 | Oakmont, Pa. |
| 1963 | *J. Boros | 293 | Brookline, Mass. |
| 1964 | K. Venturi | 278 | Congressional, D.C. |
| 1965 | *G. J. Player (SA) | 282 | Bellerive, Mo. |
| 1966 | *W. Casper | 278 | Olympic, Cal. |
| 1967 | J. Nicklaus | 275 | Baltusrol, N.J. |
| 1968 | L. Trevino | 275 | Oak Hill, N.Y. |
| 1969 | O. Moody | 281 | Champions, Texas |
| 1970 | A. Jacklin (GB) | 281 | Hazeltine, Minn. |
| 1971 | *L. Trevino | 280 | Merion, Pa. |
| 1972 | J. Nicklaus | 290 | Pebble Beach, Cal. |
| 1973 | J. Miller | 279 | Oakmont, Pa. |
| 1974 | H. Irwin | 287 | Winged Foot, N.Y. |
| 1975 | | | Medinah, Ill. |
| 1976 | | | |

*after play-off

## US Masters

*Played at Augusta National GC, Georgia.*

| *year* | *winner (US unless otherwise stated)* | *score* |
|---|---|---|
| 1946 | H. Keiser | 282 |
| 1947 | J. Demaret | 281 |
| 1948 | C. Harmon | 279 |
| 1949 | S. Snead | 283 |
| 1950 | J. Demaret | 282 |
| 1951 | B. Hogan | 280 |
| 1952 | S. Snead | 286 |
| 1953 | B. Hogan | 274 |
| 1954 | S. Snead | 289 |
| 1955 | C. Middlecoff | 279 |
| 1956 | J. Burke | 289 |
| 1957 | D. Ford | 283 |
| 1958 | A. Palmer | 284 |
| 1959 | A. Wall | 284 |
| 1960 | A. Palmer | 282 |
| 1961 | G. J. Player (SA) | 280 |

**US Masters (cont.)**

| year | winner (US unless otherwise stated) | score |
|---|---|---|
| 1962 | *A. Palmer | 280 |
| 1963 | J. Nicklaus | 286 |
| 1964 | A. Palmer | 276 |
| 1965 | J. Nicklaus | 271 |
| 1966 | *J. Nicklaus | 288 |
| 1967 | G. Brewer | 280 |
| 1968 | R. Goalby | 277 |
| 1969 | G. Archer | 281 |
| 1970 | *W. Casper | 279 |
| 1971 | C. Coody | 279 |
| 1972 | J. Nicklaus | 286 |
| 1973 | T. Aaron | 283 |
| 1974 | G. J. Player (SA) | 278 |
| 1975 | | |
| 1976 | | |

*after play-off

# USPGA

| year | winner (US unless otherwise stated) | score | venue |
|---|---|---|---|
| 1946 | B. Hogan | 6 & 4 | Portland, Ore. |
| 1947 | J. Ferrier | 2 up | Plum Hollow, Mich. |
| 1948 | B. Hogan | 7 & 6 | Norwood Hills, Mo. |
| 1949 | S. Snead | 3 & 2 | Hermitage, Va. |
| 1950 | C. Harper | 4 & 3 | Scioto, Ohio |
| 1951 | S. Snead | 7 & 6 | Oakmont, Pa. |
| 1952 | J. Turnesa | 1 up | Big Springs, Ky. |
| 1953 | W. Burkemo | 2 up | Birmingham, Mich. |
| 1954 | C. Harbert | 4 & 3 | Keller, Minn. |
| 1955 | D. Ford | 4 & 3 | Meadowbrook, Mich. |
| 1956 | J. Burke | 3 & 2 | Blue Hill, Mass. |
| 1957 | L. Hebert | 2 up | Miami Valley, Ohio |
| 1958 | D. Finsterwald | 276 | Llanerch, Pa. |
| 1959 | R. Rosburg | 277 | Minneapolis, Minn. |
| 1960 | J. Hebert | 281 | Firestone, Ohio |
| 1961 | *J. Barber | 277 | Olympia Fields, Ill. |
| 1962 | G. J. Player (SA) | 278 | Aronomink, Pa. |
| 1963 | J. Nicklaus | 279 | Dallas, Texas |
| 1964 | R. Nichols | 271 | Columbus, Ohio |
| 1965 | D. Marr | 280 | Laurel Valley, Pa. |
| 1966 | A. Geiberger | 280 | Firestone, Ohio |
| 1967 | *D. January | 281 | Columbine, Colo. |
| 1968 | J. Boros | 281 | Pecan Valley, Texas |
| 1969 | R. Floyd | 276 | Dayton, Ohio |
| 1970 | D. Stockton | 279 | Southern Hills, Okla. |
| 1971 | J. Nicklaus | 281 | Palm Beach, Fla. |
| 1972 | G. J. Player (SA) | 281 | Oakland Hills, Mich. |
| 1973 | J. Nicklaus | 277 | Canterbury, Ohio |
| 1974 | L. Trevino | 276 | Clemmons, N. C |
| 1975 | | | Akron, Ohio |
| 1976 | | | |

*after play-off

# Index

*Mr Liang-Huan Lu*

*Courses are printed in italics*

Acknowledgment is due to the following for permission to reproduce illustrations on the pages listed (on pages with more than three illustrations, illustrations are lettered a–d from the top down):

Allied Breweries, 39; Argus South African Newspapers, 121 (bottom right); Gerry Cranham, 96–7; Dunlop Limited, front cover (golf ball); Frank Gardner, back cover, 24, 25, 30, 32, 33 (right), 48, 100 (d), 105 (top and centre), 107 (c), 108 (d), 110 (b), 113 (top right and centre), 115 (top and bottom), 116 (c), 117 (right), 118 (top right), 122 (a), 123 (centre right), 125 (top), 126 (top right), 127, 134–5; Geoffrey Goddard, 2–3, 4, 8–9, 107 (d), 109 (centre left), 112 (bottom), 114 (b and d), 119 (both illustrations), 120 (top), 141; Golf Illustrated, 44; E. D. Lacey, front cover, 6, 13, 21 (left), 98 (top and bottom), 99 (d), 100 (c), 101 (all illustrations), 102 (both illustrations), 103 (b, c and d), 104 (a, b and c), 105 (bottom), 106 (d), 107 (b), 108 (a), 109 (top and bottom), 110 (a and d), 111 (all illustrations), 112 (top), 113 (top left), 114 (a and c), 116 (a and d), 117 (left), 118 (top left), 120 (centre right, centre left and bottom), 121 (top and bottom left), 122 (b, c and d), 124 (top and bottom), 125 (centre), 126 (top left and bottom); H. W. Neale, 21 (right), 46; Par Golf, 115 (centre), 118 (bottom), 123 (centre left); Press Association, 15, 22, 29, 33 (left), 42, 50, 51, 53, 54, 58, 60, 113 (bottom); US PGA, 98 (centre), 99 (a), 100 (b), 103 (a), 104 (d), 106 (a, b and c), 107 (a), 108, 110 (b and c), 116 (b), 123 (top and bottom), 125 (bottom).



Maps and diagrams by Diagram